THE
ULTIMATE
TIME MACHINE

Also by Joseph McMoneagle

Mind Trek

THE ULTIMATE TIME MACHINE

A Remote Viewer's Perception of Time,
and Predictions for the New Millennium

JOSEPH McMONEAGLE

HAMPTON ROADS
PUBLISHING COMPANY, INC.
for the evolving human spirit

Cover design by Rosie Smith/Bartered Graphics

The image on the front cover was created with support from Space Telescope
Science Institute, operated by the Association of Universities for Research in
Astronomy, Inc., from NASA contract NAS5-26555, and is reproduced here
with permission from AURA/STScI

For information write:
Hampton Roads Publishing Company, Inc.
134 Burgess Lane
Charlottesville, VA 22902

Or call: 804-296-2772
FAX: 804-296-5096

e-mail: hrpc@hrpub.com
Web site: http://www.hrpub.com

If you are unable to order this book from your local
bookseller, you may order directly from the publisher.
Quantity discounts for organizations are available.
Call 1-800-766-8009, toll-free.

Library of Congress Catalog Card Number 98-71582

ISBN 1-57174-102-X

10 9 8 7 6 5 4 3 2

Printed on acid-free recycled paper in Canada

Dedication

*This book is dedicated
to my lovely wife, Nancy,
and my very dear friend,
Ed May*

CONTENTS

PART I
STARGATE—AND REMOTE VIEWING

PART II
A VIEW OF TIME

PART III
THE NEXT ONE HUNDRED YEARS

Foreword

This may be a funny way to start a foreword, but I must admit that when I first began glancing at the manuscript for McMoneagle's *The Ultimate Time Machine*, my reaction was, frankly, less than enthusiastic. "Oh, no!" I thought, "I've agreed to write a foreword for this book because Joe's first book was so important, and now it turns out this one is all about psychic predictions of the future! These kinds of books are usually by self-styled, egotistical, and often dubious 'psychics.' They are boring, highly pessimistic (lots of predicted catastrophes as punishments for our sins and stupidities), and, from a scientific point of view, the predictions are so vaguely worded as to be meaningless and/or just plain wrong—they never come to pass. How many times has the end of the world been predicted by one psychic or another since I've been researching parapsychology, but we're still all here? What have I gotten myself into?" I could imagine other potential readers feeling the same way.

Then I stopped muttering to myself and actually read the manuscript—the sensible advice I usually give to others when I hear them complaining about something they haven't actually read. Well, my advice is pretty good, for real acquaintance with the book completely changed my reaction, and I'm now honored to be writing the foreword.

Why is this book so importantly different from the usual psychic prediction books?

First, the author, Joe McMoneagle, is not some self-styled "psychic" of dubious skill, but one of the very few people whose considerable psychic skills have been validated over and over again, validated not only in the laboratory under the strictest scientific conditions, but also validated in practical intelligence-gathering operations during his many years as a remote viewer in the United States government's classified STARGATE remote viewing program. This is not to say that any psychic who hasn't been tested in the laboratory isn't genuine, of course. There are lots of people labeled psychics out there, ranging from genuinely talented and mature people at one end of the spectrum to sincere but not so talented and somewhat deluded people in the middle range to the low end of outright charlatans who fake psychic abilities for their own gain. But there are very, very few scientists who have the interest, skills, and time to test people for psychic abilities, so Joe is a rare bird indeed to be so well validated.

Second, Joe is not egotistical; he doesn't go around putting on airs and acting special because of what he can do. The fact that I automatically think of and call him Joe, as does everyone who knows him, reminds me of that. So this book has no hidden agenda of showing off Joe's ego, which is very refreshing and makes for straightforward reading.

Third, this book is not boring. To my pleasure and amazement, Joe has not only remote viewed (a systematic and controlled form of ESP) the future occasionally, he has done so many times, kept records and systematized the results to provide a comprehensive and sophisticated vision of what the future may be like.

Note I used "may" be like, not "will" be like. As part of genuine intelligence and sensibility (Joe would probably be embarrassed if I used the word humility), Joe readily admits that both he and the remote viewing technique, while often leading to startlingly accurate psychic descriptions of the past, present and future, are also often just plain wrong. Sometimes it's clear in retrospect why the remote viewings were wrong (misleading targeting directions, for example), but we often have no idea why. In presenting his predictions, Joe makes it clear that he could be psychically wrong on some of these and that other events could change the future on some of them, so he's sharing a fascinating and thought-provoking vision of what's likely, what may be, but not an ironclad forecast of what *must* be. If this raises questions in your mind about free will and determinism—how can you predict the future unless it's fixed and we have no free will—well, those are good questions, and Joe shares some sophisticated thinking about it.

Indeed, one of the things I most liked about this book was the insightful and sophisticated psychological thinking Joe brings to life in general as well as to the area of psychic predictions. What we think is "real" is often mainly a projection of our belief systems; understanding these filters that we see through is the key to real growth.

Fourth, Joe's predictions are not simplistically pessimistic, not the "The world will end next year because you are all such miserable sinners!" style. Life is never a matter of all bad or all good, and Joe's predictions are of negative and positive changes, diseases and wars and catastrophes on the one hand, major advances in medicine and political freedom and technology on the other. This is a realism I find so lacking in most psychic predictions and in many people's interest in such predictions. It's as if we want some major catastrophe (or salvation) to happen that will take away the necessity of choice. I sometimes jocularly kid with such people that my "psychic" prediction is that the world will not end soon or be saved soon; I harshly predict that life will actually continue to go on as a mixture of good and bad, requiring us to make intelligent moral choices just like it always has! I'm just drawing on general principles, of course. Joe is intelligently aware of how such general principles affect life, but has the added advantage of being able to remote view to get specifics.

Finally, in my initial reaction I complained that most psychic predictions are too general and vague to be useful, or are just plain wrong. If you look at the prophecies of Nostradamus, for example, they tend to be fuzzily symbolic and vague as to time and what's supposed to *specifically* happen. With hindsight, you can read anything you want into them, but you don't find clear and accurate predictions like "Buy IBM in 1955." While Joe admits that some of his remote viewings of the future are vague in spite of his attempts to get clarity, a lot are much more specific. Many are far enough in the future that we will probably be dead before we know whether they are valid or not—but a fair number are scheduled for our lifetime, so we'll know. As I said above, Joe has been extensively tested and validated; we know that sometimes his remote viewings of future events are very accurate and detailed. As Joe himself admits, it's going to be very interesting to see what does and doesn't come true!

Charles T. Tart, Ph.D.

Professor, Core Faculty
Institute of Transpersonal Psychology
Palo Alto, California
Professor Emeritus of Psychology
University of California, Davis

INTRODUCTION

"Now: Ancient Rome exists, and so does Egypt and Atlantis. You not only form the future, as you think of it, but you also form the past. You have been told simple tales, and they are delightful ones; but if you were not ready to hear more you would not be in this room."

—SETH SPEAKS, Jane Roberts
Prentice-Hall, Inc., New Jersey, 1972

Since I actually view predictions about the future as an act of creation, I feel a responsibility to my fellow human beings. Stepping outside of the Unconscious Consensus and attempting to influence what might be waiting down the road, requires some degree of caution.

One of the things we have to remember when we begin to talk about the future is how emotionally attached we might be to the outcome. If I were to make a statement like "In the year 2560, there will be no more grass," a lot of readers would find that to be a very distressing statement.

However, you have to remember that by the year 2600, we may have already gone six or seven generations without grass, so it would probably not be a problem for those who are living then.

After all, how many of you miss the great herds of bison cutting across your front lawn or the sky going dark with the clouds of migrating geese?

The world is a living and breathing entity and it, too, is constantly changing. Sometimes it changes on its own; sometimes in our ignorance, we help it along. The point is that change does occur, and it is only as good or as bad as those who have to experience it want it to be.

I've had people tell me that this should not be an excuse for having allowed some of the less-than-desirable changes to take place. Aren't we guilty of poisoning the air, the water, and ground?

Yes, we are. There is no doubt about that. However, we as a species have only done what other species have done, nothing more and nothing less. We have lived, made babies, and have spread across the globe, sweeping everything in our path, then eventually, we die. So, where does our responsibility begin and end in this matter? I don't pretend to have an answer.

This is a book about time—the past, present, and future. It addresses these issues within the context of remote viewing, or making psychic predictions. Since it is impossible not to project some of my own beliefs, concerns, or feelings into the content, I haven't tried not to. I've pretty much let my feelings fall where they may. Like everyone else, I am burdened with my time and place in space.

In writing this book, I've actually developed a bit more optimism for the future. First and foremost, I believe there will be a future—maybe not the one that I would like to see, but one that I can live with. So, it seems there will always be room for compromise.

There is also strong evidence that, in general, humans ultimately try to do the right thing. In some cases, our choices may not be all that good, but we try and do whatever is best within the given circumstances.

Within this book are some very scary issues, such as runaway growth in world population, our inability to feed everyone, and our concern for the impact this might have on our future generations. There are no apparent answers. However, there appears to be a solution in the prediction of a world that does not have the numbers we have today. One should not automatically jump to a conclusion that a terrible calamity is necessary to bring population growth under control. Because there are eight billion fewer people in the year 3000 does not necessary *guarantee* a devastating plague of mythic proportions. The answer might be found in the discovery of a new form of transportation that will allow us to resettle on Earth-type worlds hundreds of light years away. It might also reside in simple attrition over a thousand years of sane policy, based on good sense and pragmatic decision making.

The point I'm trying to make here is that you shouldn't automatically jump to a conclusion based on anything you read here. Instead, allow yourself to become open to the possibilities. Use the knowledge you might garner from this book to be creative in developing your own day-to-day solutions to problems, and in your interactions with others. The solution to the problems we face are within us, but they won't be accessible to a closed mind, or a frightened one.

This book talks about time: how and why the past can be changed as easily as our clothing; why the present probably doesn't exist; and how we can manipulate our future. I don't present the information in a way that provides answers, but hopefully in a way that demands thought. In some cases, I might even come across as subtly trying to provoke the reader.

A large portion of the book is filled with very specific predictions. Some people will agree with some of them and some people won't. Of course I'm hoping for both.

Finally, there is a chapter on the year 3000—a world as far from us in time as a neighboring star. Or is it?

As removed as the year 3000 may seem to be, we had a lot in common with those who lived a thousand years before we arrived. We can see very little difference in us or in our ancestors.

In the year 1000, kings and emperors ruled great cities—Otto III moved into Rome, King Rajaraja conquered Ceylon, and Olaf I died in battle making Norway Danish.

Beowulf was written in old English, and *The Pillow-Book of Sei Shonagon*, the diary of a woman in the Imperial Court of Japan, was forbidden literature.

Fresco and mosaic paintings became the rage in Italy, art and science flourished in Ghazni, the Abbey of St. Hilaire, in Poitiers. The Mayan civilization abruptly ended on the Yucatan peninsula; Leif Ericson discovered North America; and an Indian by the name of Sridhara recognized the significance of zero. And . . . there was widespread fear that the end of the world and the last judgment day was upon the human race.

There is also a hidden element in this book. It's a secret formula written between the lines, and probably the most important message the book carries. This book is about a philosophic viewpoint, one that comes and goes throughout history, but that never seems to stick.

We are ultimately responsible for reality itself, a consequence of our thoughts, words, and actions. So it is about the power and battle of consciousness, our relationship with the Grand Engineer, and our responsibilities for what our future will contain.

One additional note is required. There are some issues I do not address within this book, which some will feel should be addressed. An example would be the Y2K problem, or what is going to happen as a result of the computer chip date malfunction, in the year 2000. So, deciding what should go into this book was a significant issue from the outset.

To solve this dilemma, I decided that I would not address those issues which in themselves were already well-known. In other words, since we know there is going to be a problem with computers and chips in the New Year 2000, and we know why, simple logic should suggest appropriate actions that need to be taken, and therefore it should be unnecessary for me to address it.

Joseph W. McMoneagle
Nellysford, Virginia

PART I

STARGATE— AND REMOTE VIEWING

1

TIME AND FUTURE VISION

Some of you may have already heard about STAR-GATE, the secret government program that used remote viewers. The classified program was designed and developed by the United States Army for the specific purpose of using military intelligence personnel as psychics, to collect intelligence and to evaluate the degree to which our enemies might be capable of using psychics against us.

Normally I wouldn't feel a need to do more than just touch on the details of the remote viewing program but, unfortunately, the media blitz that followed the exposure of STARGATE resulted in a plethora of statements about remote viewing that were filled with inaccuracies and disinformation. Most of it contained very little information about what remote viewing actually is or is capable of.

There have been long and airy dissertations regarding the appropriate or inappropriate "methods" of remote viewing that are now accepted as representing the scientific protocols. Numerous statements about the accuracy of remote viewing and remote viewers have been made that do not even come close to the findings generated by twenty-five years of research in support of remote viewing science. These inaccuracies, along with gross exaggerations regarding real remote viewing capabilities, leave me very little option but to comment.

It would take almost an entire book to address the huge volume of misconceptions, so I've chosen only from those areas that apply to the subject at hand—time and future vision.

A Brief History of STARGATE

Originally titled GRILLFLAME, STARGATE began in 1978. It was originally based on the results of experimentation at SRI-International from 1972 through 1975 under the auspices of the CIA and other agencies. Because of those findings and publications, a proposal was made by elements within the United States Army Intelligence and Security Command to recruit, attempt to train, and utilize psychics for the collection of intelligence information. I was one of the original six viewers recruited. I was known as Remote Viewer 001. Over the next seventeen years, the project was renamed CENTER LANE. When the project was moved to the Defense Intelligence Agency (DIA) in the late 1980s, its name was changed to SUN STREAK, and finally STARGATE.

I was assigned to the unit as an intelligence officer and remote viewer from 1978 through the latter part of 1984, at which time I retired from the military. Following my retirement, I was hired as a consultant to the Research and Development portion of the project, which was located at SRI-International. It was there that I continued to provide support as a viewer for both intelligence collection as well as the research efforts. I moved with the Cognitive Science Laboratory (CSL) at SRI-International to Science Applications International Corporation in 1991 and stayed with the project until its termination in November 1995. While not the longest-surviving viewer with the project, I am certainly one of two or three who went the distance.

Contrary to popular belief, and like nearly all experimental projects, it was never 100 percent successful. However, during its full operational period, I know that we did provide information of critical intelligence value in hundreds of very specific cases. On scores of occasions, this information was also described within government documents as being un-available from any other source(s).

Also contrary to popular belief, the program operated throughout its history under the very watchful eyes of numerous oversight committees, which were both scientific and governmental. During the seventeen and a half years it ran, it provided support to nearly all of the United States intelligence agencies. Its very existence was approved on a year-to-year basis by these committees and agencies and it was judged and funded not only by its successes, but according to how well it operated within the rules and scientific boundaries set by those agencies and oversight committees. Any suggestion that the program operated loosely, or with a lack of control, is pure bunk. To understand why such bogus rumors persist, one must understand that, historically, it suffered, and suffered greatly, from the inability of those within management to deal with its nature. It was a political, social, and managerial hot potato. "Put it in anyone's back yard except mine!" Or to put it in the elegant terms of a very good friend, who still swims in the upper crust of government, "Nobody has the guts to admit they fear it."

As a consequence, many people have become bogged down in arguing the percentages of success in using psychics, a false measure by anyone's account. What's important to understand here is that by the time we received a mission, all other intelligence attempts, methods, or approaches had already been exhausted.

The practice of alternative medicine provides a good analogy. Having exhausted all traditional medical practices, a patient has usually been declared terminally ill and without hope by the time s/he walks through the door of an alternative medicine practitioner. In such cases, even a recovery rate of 15 to 20 percent would be considered miraculous.

In context, we viewed a remote viewing success rate of 60 percent as pretty remarkable.

The project was closed in November of 1995, when the American Institutes for Research filed an unclassified report with Congress. That report had been written at the request of Congress and the CIA. I believe that the report is totally bogus. Those interested in understanding why can read about it in Chapter 21 of my revised edition of *Mind Trek* (Hampton Roads Publishing, 1997).

The largest portion of the project papers (95 percent) are still classified and lie within more than a hundred sealed boxes in a government basement somewhere in Washington, D.C. If or when those documents might be declassified is anyone's guess.

However, the research lives on. Since termination of the project in 1995, I have continued as a research associate with CSL, now located in Palo Alto, California. We still do research and pursue the hidden answers to why or how remote viewing works.

After twenty years of effort, I still do not pretend to understand, nor do I claim to know all that can be known about it. But to set the record straight, here are some things we *do* know.

Protocols

Many people don't understand what the word "protocol" means. In spite of the fact that remote viewing should always be performed within an accepted scientific protocol, there are those who call themselves remote viewers even though they don't have a clue what a protocol is.

According to Merriam Webster's Collegiate Dictionary, Tenth Edition, a protocol is a "detailed plan of a scientific or medical experiment, treatment, or procedure."

The protocols, or procedures, used within the intelligence collection or applications side of Project STARGATE were developed and based on the remote viewing protocols designed, tested, and developed within the research side of that project. This research was accomplished at SRI-International from 1972 through 1991, at Science Applications International Corporation from 1991 through 1995, and is continuing at the Cognitive Sciences Laboratory, Palo Alto, California.

These protocols are the same ones now being used at other labs located in England, Germany, South America, Russia, and Hungary. Some of the most notable are

- The Koestler Chair of Parapsychology, Department of Psychology, University of Edinburgh, Scotland

- The Princeton Engineering Anomalies Research (PEAR) Laboratory, Princeton University

- The Department of Psychology at the University of Amsterdam

- The Rhine Research Center, Durham, North Carolina

One does not have to be involved with one of these institutes or labs to design or produce a protocol. In other words, you do not need a "Dr." in front of your name to construct a protocol. It is also wise to remember that having a Dr. in front of a name doesn't guarantee you are faultless when you do.

Regardless of source, a protocol is not a valid protocol unless

- it is published (usually within a study)

- it is open to peer review and criticism

These requirements are generally ignored by many who are now claiming expertise in the "development" of such protocols and the scientific controls associated with remote viewing. Surprisingly, there are even some laboratories that violate these principals.

Protocols used for remote viewing have a number of requirements that must be met. These are usually nonnegotiable, or if changed, are only done so after years of study. Generally, the protocol must ensure the following:

> The target is totally blind to the remote viewer.

> The target is totally blind to the facilitator or monitor (person in the room with the remote viewer, if any).

> The person who may be judging or evaluating the results does not participate in any other portion of the remote viewing.

> The person who selects the target for remote viewing does not participate in any other portion of the remote viewing experiment or in the attempt at information collection.

While these rules may appear to be extreme, they aren't. They exist to ensure that real "psychic functioning" is taking place and not something that simply looks like it.

For example, if someone knows what the target is and is sitting in the room with the remote viewer during the remote viewing, even as an observer, they are communicating something about the target, the correctness of the response, or otherwise affecting the process. Human beings do not communicate by voice alone. A raised eyebrow, the way we shift in a chair, the actions of our hands and arms, even our head movements or the workings of our jawline when we clench our teeth, speak volumes of information about what may or may not be correct about what the viewer is saying. Since most of these nonverbal actions are subconscious, we don't even know we are communicating or passing information.

So, by necessity, the use of an appropriate protocol for the production of information by remote viewing must follow strict and unforgiving guidelines if we are to guarantee the information to be psychic. There are no exceptions.

Front-loading

As a result of many stories regarding the applications of remote viewing, specifically those addressing its use within Project STARGATE, a number of myths have evolved and have recently become popular. One of these deals with front-loading.

Front-loading is a belief that a remote viewer must be told something about the target for him or her to obtain information about it. This is not true.

In the case of researchers using remote viewing within a lab, front-loading is never allowed. There are no exceptions.

Within applications, or when remote viewing is being used to collect information on a subject or topic that is inherently unknown in the beginning, confusion has arisen as a result of not differentiating between material used to "target" a remote viewer and the type or style of information that would be considered front-loading.

When a specific target has been chosen for an application of remote viewing, there has to be a means for centering the remote viewer on the actual target. This is commonly referred to as targeting material(s).

As an example, if you want to know what kind of a machine an unknown engineer is in the process of building, there are a number of ways to target a remote viewer without telling him or her.

You could use a photograph of the engineer as the targeting mechanism, obtain a physical-location coordinate for the machine, or even use the photograph of the exterior of the building in which the machine is being constructed. Ideally, you would put these items inside a sealed envelope and ask the remote viewer to provide information concerning the target contained within the envelope.

However, if the individual in the photograph or at the location is totally unknown to the remote viewer and monitor, then actually handing them the coordinates for the location, or the individual's photograph, along with instructions to describe what's inside the building may be appropriate. In such a case it would be considered a form of "targeting."

Some argument can be made that the size of the building infers what the target might "not" be, but this is a reach. Anyone in the military program who was targeted against a prototype "tank" hidden in an "aircraft hanger" can attest to that.

In a way, this does front-load the remote viewer with something connected to the actual target, but it isn't considered front-loading in the negative sense that you are telling them what you are specifically looking for.

A good remote viewer will eventually tell you something about the "machine" during the course of the remote viewing session, because that is the expectation of everyone participating in the collection effort, not because they were told what kind of machine it was.

However, if you ask a remote viewer to "describe a machine" identified within a sealed envelope, or connected to the photograph, or the coordinates, then you are front-loading the remote viewer with the concept of a machine. That is not acceptable.

It's really very simple. If you are saying anything to the remote viewer that directly identifies what you are interested in, or that gives any hint of what the actual subject of the remote viewing might be, you are front-loading inappropriately.

As another example, let's look at a building as a target. It is obvious that sometimes a photograph of the exterior of a building says something about what is going on inside it. It may be the building's name embossed on the side, flags hanging on the outside, the types of or even lack of windows, the position of security cameras, the fencing, guard uniforms, even how close one is permitted to park to the actual facility. In this case, a proper "targeting" photograph might be a section or fragment of the building's roof, a snapshot of the actual entry or a doorway, from which all other data has been cropped.

Front-loading, on the other hand, would be any photograph that says something about what the facility might be, what it does, who works there, etc.

The difference between good "targeting" material and what would be considered front-loading is sometimes a very fine line. Making such a decision is generally applicable only to applications types of targets, and it should be left to an expert in remote viewing. Even then, mistakes are made. In the event anyone believes a remote viewer has been front-loaded, the information should be abandoned, as it is no longer being produced through psychic functioning and therefore holds no value as psychic information, since its point of origin can no longer be determined.

Front-loading is the most common source of contamination in a remote viewing session and is never tolerated by anyone, especially a professional remote viewer. Front-loading is an easy mistake to make, since far less focus is paid to the person setting up the target than the viewer, when it should be just the opposite.

To put this into contemporary terms, let's take the Comet Hale-Bopp as a target. How would you approach this problem?

Any coordinate system used (right ascension/declination) would be quickly recognized as being celestial, so that is out of the question. Any mention of the comet's name or how it is codified or referenced by astronomers is easily accessed and available, and as such would probably be recognized, so that is out as well. This is especially true of anyone who has an immediate interest in the Comet in the first place. You could expect them to have read all the available news and commentary about it. If they have, then everything they've read or heard becomes a heavy possibility for contaminating the results if there is even the slightest hint that Hale-Bopp might be their target.

What if you are someone who is known to be interested

in celestial targets? In other words, it is common knowledge that you are interested in comets, asteroids, or possibly UFOs. Just knowing that you are the person who selected the target will sway some viewer's perceptions and taint the process, causing them to give you what you want to hear.

The only way you could process this target properly would be to place it within a target pool that has no large component of other targets of a similar nature. This means there could not be a lot of other asteroids, comets, planets, or UFOs within the target pool.

The target pool would also have to be large enough to preclude any possible guessing on the part of an individual remote viewer. Targets would have to be chosen randomly from the pool, and you would have to wait until that particular envelope was chosen to get your answers. The actual target material itself (the name Hale-Bopp) would have to be kept sealed within the envelope until after all the remote viewing or information collection has been completed. In other words, it would have to be kept blind to all participants until after the remote viewing has taken place. In truth, the smaller a target pool is, the more difficult it is for the remote viewer. One is more likely to remember the multitude of targets contained within a small pool. While it is true that it is impossible to know which target has been selected if they are in sealed envelopes, it does not preclude one from thinking about all of the targets in the pool, which clouds the mind with useless information, 90 percent of which is not pertinent to the actual target. It actually makes the viewing effort tougher for the participant.

Multiple Viewers

Another myth regarding remote viewing is that multiple viewers are better, more accurate, or increase the possibility of accuracy through consensus. This is already appearing in print in a number of periodicals and books. It is probably born out of numerous observations that took place during the STARGATE program. While observations may automatically lead to assumptions, such observations do not inherently make these assumptions correct.

It is true that more than one viewer was usually targeted against a specific target. It is also true that more than one viewer might have even produced "like" information on any specific target, and at times, this information might have been correct. However, what is not true is that the use of multiple viewers or their consensus on any specific target would in any way guarantee the accuracy or improve the information they were providing.

Over two decades of research fails to support multiple viewer accuracy as an appropriate conclusion. In fact, the results of such research tend to flow in the opposite direction.

If you are using multiple viewers, the one or two viewers who differ from the majority view are just as likely to be the ones that are providing the correct information.

Time and again, when there was 80-90 percent consensus, the consensus group proved to be wrong. While it is difficult to tell what might be the cause for this during research, it isn't so difficult to see why it happens sometimes within applications. The culprit will usually be the type of material that was used to target the different viewers. It was either so close to bordering on front-loading that they all responded as expected, or the front-loading occurred but was not recognized. I've always referred to this as accidental front-loading.

Accidental front-loading is an interesting topic, since it really hasn't been heavily investigated by anyone. The way it probably operates is something like the following:

I am the facilitator or monitor for six remote viewers. We are all blind to the target. The targeting mechanism is considered valid, since it is only a photograph of a plain, smooth-surfaced door, otherwise unidentifiable. As a monitor or facilitator, I am given the instruction "We want to know what's behind the door." (Note: Perhaps what they really want to know is how the people behind the door are dressed, or where the elevator is located.)

The first viewer produces lots of detail about what appears to be some kind of an office. The second viewer does the same, as well as the third, fourth, and fifth. The sixth becomes argumentative and describes what appears to be an elevator shaft, with uniformed guards.

The myth is assuming viewers one through five are correct by consensus, when in fact the location of the elevator and existence of guards is what is being sought. So, we only have to take a closer look at the events to see how this could happen.

As the monitor, even though I didn't know what the target was, *because* I was the monitor for *all* the remote viewers and believed the perceptions of the first viewer to be somewhat true, I was already assuming what the others would be telling me beginning with viewer number two.

As soon as I gave weight to the first viewer's perceptions and images (even if only subconsciously), I then began delivering subtle impressions regarding the target to the remaining five vis-à-vis the content or framing of my questions, or perhaps through body language. Only the sixth viewer seemingly displayed exceptional viewing ability, and rather than operate off my nonverbal cues or messages, chose to stick with his raw or psychic impressions.

So perhaps we need to add another rule to the remote viewing protocol (at least regarding application types of targets).

> ➤ Never use the same monitor or facilitator with multiple remote viewers on the same target.

Historically, both the research and applications fail to statistically support a reality that multiple viewers will increase the amount or the degree of accuracy about a specific target. To state otherwise at the present time would be unwise.

Target Selected by Viewer

Within research, the only way a viewer should select his or her own target is indirectly. For example, viewers can access the numbers of targeted envelopes using random number generators. The envelopes themselves should never be turned over to the viewer, and the viewers should never have access to the target pool once it's been constructed (targets have been placed in the envelopes).

The reason for this is to preclude marking or otherwise surreptitiously identifying target envelopes. Many interpret this as a lack of trust and balk at participating in experiments where such controls exist. However, these controls are not meant to denigrate the honest remote viewer, and they are certainly not exercised to cast an unfavorable light on any viewer.

It has taken years of effort and perseverance to establish parapsychology as a valid and sophisticated science. Throughout those years, a number of cases of fraud were observed and uncovered. While these cases are rare, the damage done to the credibility of the science is incalculable. Because of the high "giggle factor" associated with paranormal research especially by the ignorant and misinformed, when fraud is discovered, the effects are far more devastating than when they occur in other areas of science.

An article exposing an aeronautical engineer for falsifying research data hardly rates a back page in the local newspaper, but perpetuate deliberate fraud in a parapsychology experiment, and it doesn't die out for months, even years in some cases.

Efforts taken to prevent fraud do not imply something is wrong with an individual's character or integrity. It has everything to do with protecting everyone involved in the research, to include the viewers. Efforts should be established to eradicate the possibility of fraud wherever it might be possible. It is part of the viewer's responsibility to point out weaknesses within the process wherever or whenever they are noticed.

While there is focus and pressure on science to prevent fraud, I must sadly report that this is not true with many of those involved in remote viewing outside of the lab. Numerous facilities have sprung up around the world that are purportedly using remote viewing for applications, as well as teaching it. It is impossible to determine to what degree they are following the rules, establishing safeguards, or guaranteeing the appropriate controls for the prevention of fraud. One has to walk through the door and purchase services, or training, then judge for oneself.

These comments should not be misconstrued as derogatory to those establishments that have such controls in place, nor does it imply that all establishments are sloppy.

My own company, Intuitive Intelligence Applications, has been tested on more than one occasion. It is the primary reason I have accepted numerous challenges to do a remote viewing under strict controls—while being filmed. Five of eight attempts have been successful, and two were blown targets (in one case we did not get to a precognitive target site in time to film and in the second I was not allowed inside the selected target for feedback). The two most notable successes were the ABC special "Put to the Test," and a remote viewing filmed for Reader's Digest Home Video at the Rhine Research Center titled; "Mysteries of the Unexplained, Powers of the Paranormal."

Other Myths

Remote Viewers Can Be Blocked

There is no evidence that this true. In fact, since 1979 there have been numerous attempts at shielding targets from remote viewers. Attempts to shield targets have always been viewed as a possible back door toward understanding the mechanisms that might underlie the transfer of information. If we are able to shield remote viewers in some way, then the types of shielding and the effectiveness of shielding will say a lot about what the mechanisms might be for the delivery of the information—something akin to backing in the door through reverse engineering.

Some data suggests that certain electromagnetic noise environments may have an effect on remote viewing, but these are not conclusive. Neither positive nor negative shielded cages have had a decisive effect.

I believe that shielding is possible, but only when using a combination of things/techniques not yet explored. There are times when remote viewing just doesn't seem to work on its own. If researchers are ever able to connect those times to specific environmental elements or events, I'm sure an answer will be just around the corner.

A lot has been said about aliens being able to block remote viewing. This may or may not be true. Since there is no formal contact with aliens who will agree to participate in formal remote viewing experiments, there is no way to ensure the validity of such a statement. It will have to remain in the "unknown" category. Saying it doesn't make it so, nor does saying it make it go away.

Feedback on a Target Isn't a Requirement

Some say that without feedback about a target you might as well be writing science fiction.

There has been enough study in remote viewing, however, to state that feedback may not be a requirement for the remote viewer to perform. There have been remote viewings accomplished by viewers who died prior to receiving their feedback. The results of these viewings were statistically consistent with other remote viewings the viewers did while alive. So, feedback in the formal sense, that it needs to occur for remote viewing to take place, is not necessarily the case.

However, feedback is absolutely essential for judging or evaluating a report for accuracy. If I were randomly targeted against a UFO event that took place at a specific time and place in the past, I might provide information that appears to be consistent with the event, but this does not in itself guarantee accuracy across the board with regard to the information I have provided.

In fact, I was targeted against a UFO sighting that was witnessed by nearly two thousand people in Tacoma, Washington, in the 1950s. The witnesses reported "dancing lights in the sky."

The target was a newspaper clipping that had been placed within an envelope and that was placed within a larger target pool (of more than two hundred targets). It was one of only two or three UFO targets within the pool. The target was chosen randomly some weeks later by a hand-held random number generator.

My first statement in the remote viewing room was "I see lights dancing on the horizon." This was followed by a spontaneous out-of-body experience, wherein I saw and interacted with an apparition of my father, who had died three years earlier, and a multilight, humanoid-shaped entity.

Was this a confirmation of contact with an alien?

No. And it should not be misconstrued as such.

It did confirm the UFO-related target—the dancing lights. As regards the other events, I haven't got the foggiest idea what was going on and neither does anyone else. I've never had any feedback. So, the balance of the experience will, at this time, have to be labeled "unknown" and is not conclusive proof for anything.

On the other hand, if a multilight, humanoid-shaped entity makes contact with the Oval Office and a picture is plastered across the front page of the *Washington Post*, then I've got the validation for a much larger chunk of the remote viewing session as having been correct.

There are numerous targets for which I have not received any feedback, simply because there wasn't any. For other targets, the feedback came in later, in some cases as much as eight or nine years later. While it is a remarkable experience, to receive feedback that validates something you said in a remote viewing session eight or nine years earlier, the material is still "unknown" for that eight or nine years it sat in a file.

There are exceptions to this. On occasion, we will receive information that is currently "unknown" about a target or location, but this may provide a reason for going to find out. If I remote viewed the location of a diamond mine and said that it was located in Aunt Zelda's flower garden, few would wait for the feedback. They'd more than likely be out there digging up Aunt Zelda's flowers.

This is one of the strange and unique differences between a research target and an applications target. Within research, the target will either be correctly described or it won't be. If it is described properly, it's a hit. If it isn't, then it is a miss. Within the applications area, it may at first glance appear to be uncorroborated information and a miss. By providing the information, however, this sometimes generates an action, or ensures that one is taken, that sometimes produces further feedback, which proves the accuracy of the remote viewing in the first place. In some cases it becomes hard to tell which is the chicken and which is the egg.

An example of this occurred within Project STARGATE. In 1979, we provided information on a building in the north of the Soviet Union, where we stated quite emphatically that the Soviets were building a new class of submarine. There was no data existent to confirm this, nor did many other agencies agree with us at the time. However, we also provided information on when the new submarine would probably be launched.

As a result, photographs were eventually obtained of the never-before-seen Typhoon class submarine, which validated our information, and at that point, the remote viewing information was considered to be correct. Bottom line: feedback is always essential for knowing if the remote viewing information is accurate or not.

This feedback loop has a considerable impact on future targets. (See discussion on page 119.) Future targeting can sometimes turn the whole process on its ear.

There Are Different Kinds of Remote Viewing

Remote viewing is subject to being performed within an approved protocol. Numerous protocols have been developed, each with its own brand of target access or control. Some of these include the following:

➤ **Outbounder targeting.** This is where a targeted individual actually travels to a target location and interacts with the target while they are being targeted. Generally speaking, this increases the remote viewer's perceived contact with the target. It is primarily used for research, but can on occasion be used for applications purposes as well as training.

➤ **Coordinate target.** Geographic, map grid, military, and other forms of coordinates (encrypted or unencrypted) were used in the very early years of the STARGATE project, but this practice has nearly been abandoned. While it is effective, a lot of questions were raised regarding eidetic memory and the possibility of fraud. Most of the arguments against using a system of coordinates for targeting do not hold water. But since there are other just as effective methods available, there is no sense in arguing about it.

➤ **Sealed envelopes.** Probably one of the most common forms of targeting. You can put names, locations, addresses, photographs, almost anything relating to a specific target of interest within a sealed and opaque envelope. You can then put the envelope on a desk in front of the viewer, or you can put it in another room, another state, or halfway across the country.

➤ **Numeric/alphabetic keys.** This technique assigns a randomly chosen set of digits, characters, or mixture of both to a target of interest, then uses the sequence to access the target. There are inherent problems with this technique. Unless one keeps a permanent list of all combinations used previously for all viewers, you won't know if you are using the same combination twice. A specific sequence or key should only be used once to identify a single target. Targets stored in computer systems are generally selected in this manner.

The above descriptions represent changes in method of targeting and are therefore changes to the original protocol designed for remote viewing. Almost any change in targeting will alter the protocol, and therefore must be looked at very carefully before being employed.

The titles *technical, controlled, scientific, advanced, altered state, natural,* or *guided* are terms used to identify some of the "methods" of remote viewing employed. Remember, methods are only as good as the protocol within which they operate. If the methods are not performed within accepted remote viewing protocol, they have neither scientific nor applications validity.

Numerous methods have been developed over the past twenty years. At least a half dozen methods (if not more) were adopted within the STARGATE program itself, most of which have been used to one extent or another within the research side of the program as well. To date, there is no research or applications evidence to suggest that one method was better than another with regard to remote viewing consistency or accuracy. In fact, some of the methods might have done more damage than good.

There have since been a number of methods developed outside of the STARGATE program, which some claim as being "newer" or "better." Since they have not met the test of fire within a research lab, or have not been open to peer review and criticism, I will make no comment about them or their validity.

Additionally, since the reality of remote viewing is fully dependent on the method (no matter which) being used within the constraints of an approved protocol, any method used can be called remote viewing as long as it works within a valid protocol.

Numerous complaints have appeared in print recently that people are attempting to use channeling, tarot cards, crystal balls, tea leaves, candles, meditation, out-of-body travel, astral projection, etc., as a means or method for producing remote viewing information. The inference is that this somehow invalidates that remote viewing is taking place. It does not. If someone wants to wrap themselves in an orange sheet, hum Dixie through their left nostril, while writing the information down backward in archaic Greek, that's fine. I don't know how well they might do, but as long as they do it within an approved remote viewing protocol, it is still considered remote viewing.

Likewise, producing good information within an approved or strict remote viewing protocol only proves that psychic functioning has taken place, and does not in any way validate the efficacy of scrying, throwing bones, or tarot card reading.

Obviously, there may be constraints that arise from the use of some methods that may interfere with the remote viewing protocol. In such a case where a conflict between the two arises, the method would have to be abandoned—but never the protocol. There are persons and establishments that historically defend their "method" as a protocol. Clearly they have missed the boat with regard to remote viewing.

How Many Viewers Were There Anyway?

In the entire history of the sponsored program, there are only a couple of offices within the government that actually provided remote viewers, and all of the viewing for record was done within Project STARGATE.

Aside from those labs listed at the beginning of this Appendix, there were only a couple of laboratories that actually participated in remote viewing research prior to 1995. Only one of those was funded with government money, or had direct access to the STARGATE program—the Cognitive Sciences Laboratory (CSL).

The total number of remote viewers within the STARGATE program will never be known, unless all the records are declassified. However, it would be more than safe to say that throughout its history, there were less than two dozen qualified viewers. And . . . they all knew one another.

PART II

A VIEW OF TIME

2

TIME

Throughout history, time has meant a lot of different things to a lot of people. It's been a place in history, an event marker, a healer, sometimes fleeting, sometimes stretched far beyond our sight. It's old beyond reason, newly born, the length of a prayer or a hope, shared or unshared. Time is something we blame wrinkles on. We wait on time, share the time, and use it to make sure our eggs are done. Time is integral to how we recognize events, when they start and when they end, birthdays, anniversaries, and deaths. Time tells us something about where we are in relation to the things we've experienced, are participating in, or have yet to imagine, whether we liked them or not. Sometimes we even run out of it.

Time is important to each and every one of us. It allows us to put things in perspective. It permits us to share information with others in a way that we can all understand, in a way that supports our general consensus or agreements about reality and, more specifically, how we think reality might operate.

A formal definition of time can be found in any dictionary. The tenth edition of *Merriam Webster's Collegiate Dictionary* defines time in this way: "1 a. the measured or measurable period during which an action, process, or condition exists or continues . . . b. a nonspatial continuum that is measured in terms of events which succeed one another from past through present to future."

But is it? Does action have to occur in the present to create the past? Can the future be predicted when it hasn't yet happened? Is there really something called the present?

To address the past, present, or future, we have to first establish what those words mean. All three apply, or are related to, *time*. Everyone's perceptions of what time might mean will vary, based on what they have experienced, were taught, or believe. Perception of time will nearly always be the way in which it directly relates to our own more personal view of life and how we have come to know something. In fact, most the-sauruses provide another word for time—"life."

So, we either view time as the *brackets* that encapsulate a single or complete event within our lives, like a birth, death, or football game. Or it is a summation of events, a linear string of happenings that represent a specific period or dura-tion—like our school years, time spent in the military, or on a vacation.

Clearly these definitions lend great support to many of the scientific views about time and how it functions within reality. Time limits, fences, or brackets observed events, thereby helping to quantify the relationships that might exist between them. Where groups of events occur, one can ob-serve them in a linear fashion, and in some cases, see the cause-and-effect relationships between them. This gives rise to a belief that somehow time flows, and even more uniquely, always it seems, in a singular direction.

While such simplistic definitions might support normal human processing or maybe our own actions as they might relate to our existence, I believe that time is a far more complex issue than we know. Within the components of time, additional factors exist, which have not yet surfaced. There is probably some "X" factor, if not "Y" and "Z" factors, that have until recently remained hidden from us.

To understand how time operates, we must first evaluate our meanings for and relationship to the past, present, and future, and what effect they might have on us as cognitive beings. As a remote viewer, these have come to represent entire new concepts for me.

A common view of the past, present, and future states that we can evaluate each separately and that their operating parameters are pretty much fixed, at least within reality as we understand it.

a. The past has happened. It can't be undone, so therefore it can't be changed. The past is and always will be irrefutable or fixed.

b. The present is happening as we speak, and we clearly have some control over it through the expression of free will.

c. The future hasn't happened yet, so no one really knows anything about it. While sometimes we can make a reasonable guess about the future, it is generally not very predictable, and we will usually be surprised by it.

Most people would agree that when we talk about the past, we are referring to an event or period of time that, in our perception, has already happened. Dealing with an event in the present suggests that it is occurring in the now, or that it is being perceived as it unfolds or happens. And the future? Well, we normally don't even address the future except in the hypothetical, because everyone assumes it hasn't yet occurred.

The need to create a linear perception of time—past, present, and future—probably has something to do with how we process information. But this belies the complexity of the web lying just beneath the surface. I believe the strands of this web tie all events—past, present, or future—together, creating a holistic construct we call reality. A slight tug on the end of any one part of the web shakes the whole, and changes the very fabric of reality as we understand it. So, if we are ever to make sense of this, we'll have to look at the entire web from a new perspective.

3

THE PAST

When you think about an event (time) or a period of connective events (also time) that occurred in the past, there is a perception that time is fixed. It can't be changed. The reasons for such a perception are easily understood.

Setting the subject of reincarnation aside for the moment (this will be addressed in a later chapter), and looking only at conscious awareness and memory, we all enter reality as a nearly clean slate. At the moment of our birth we have no past, other than what we've been able to process during our development in the womb.

Beginning with our moment of conception, we systematically begin to collect a past, which we store in memory. After physical birth, the information we collect, or come to believe, is then heavily moderated or controlled, first by our senses—what we see, hear, taste, smell, or feel—then by outside influences, initially our parents, then our siblings, peers, teachers, church, government, and environment. These are the influential and educational methods or facilities that have been created consciously and unconsciously, to teach us what is supposed to be fact, what is real, what is known versus unknown. These formal and informal establishments go to a great deal of trouble to deliver their information to us and we pretty much assume the information is accurate. Eventually we even come to call the information "knowledge," which implies "knowing," as opposed to "believing." So we generally accept the knowledge as truth, and delegate our beliefs to a category we might call "less than adequate."

Why is belief on the bottom of the pile? It's because we are human, curious, and constantly thinking a great deal about almost everything. As a result, we store more than we will ever need. As our memories build, larger and larger files fill with knowledge. We have to maintain some degree of control over all this information or go crazy, so we become more and more selective about what we are willing to hang on to. Eventually we have to begin chucking some of it out. We hang on to those things we have labeled "known," and pitch the stuff labeled "believe." Over time, our world becomes more and more fixed.

Eventually, our willingness to accept new facts narrows to such a point that it literally takes an "in-your-face situation" or what I call "a penetrating and life-core shock to the system" to produce change.

Such determined and resolute narrow-mindedness can't possibly be automatic. It must also be driven by some inner need.

I believe it is a major defense mechanism. It's there because of our natural desire for security, a safe and protected space.

Within us resides the known. Outside of us resides the dark, the unknown, that which we inherently fear. By inventing and understanding the past and how it might relate to us as individuals, we make ourselves comfortable and secure.

But this can *only* work if the past is unchanging and fixed, providing us with a clear understanding of who and what we are within the context of time/reality. An unchanging past supports our current actions. If we compare our current actions with the past and view them as new or different, it even implies progress. It gives us a sense of security and demonstrates an ability to grow. It will always make us better and more competent than our forefathers. They did a pretty good job, but we do better.

By demonstrating that we are able to improve on the past, we are being responsible, wise, and judicious. We are making things better. We are in control.

Science is very supportive of this "knowing." Archaeology, anthropology, and theology create intricate histories that come into play, representing "observational" records that now go back millennia. However, unless we are a trained researcher or historian, and have focused on some specific or narrow aspect of history, we ourselves can't know. We can only accept what has been written or taught as fact. And we usually do this simply because someone says it is so. But is it?

During the months I spent working on this book, many of my perceptions of the past changed. I have observed that the experts have proven that dinosaurs were warm-blooded, then cold-blooded again. Science determined that Neanderthal and Cro-Magnon man lived in caves, side by side, but they did not mate. Then someone said they mated and then not mated again. Some believe that life does not exist on other planets, then it does, then it doesn't again.

Not surprisingly, there is even evidence that the past wasn't really as fixed in the past as the past is today. At one point we were absolutely assured the Sun revolved around the Earth, then just as mysteriously it no longer did.

Of course the point I am trying to make is that the past (history) is not as fixed as we would like it to be. It is probably more of a "variable." The degree of variability is determined based on just how far back we might be going from what we perceive as now, where we are currently standing from a religious, social, or political viewpoint, and what our perception is as regards time.

Let's make it more personal.

Imagine your past as beginning with the last great moment or event you experienced. For sake of argument, let's assume the event was an accident that produced some kind of pain.

One can argue that this event or moment will be pretty much fixed in time, and it probably is, at least in the way a single individual (the one experiencing the event) might perceive it. Since it is a more personalized experience, an observation that belongs only to you (the observer), it is burned into your consciousness. There it will remain, more or less fixed. At least until one departs from reality.

Does this make it any more real for the rest of us? Probably not.

Even if you wrote down your experience, there would always be someone who would argue with you about what you meant at the time you wrote it. And if you die, that really complicates matters, since you are no longer here to defend what you wrote.

A prime example of this might be the quatrains of Nostradamus. While there seems to be general agreement that he was probably making predictions, the specifics of those predictions are, and always have been, completely open to interpretation. Some people take them literally, while others read a great deal into them. Is one person right and one person wrong? It's hard to say. Proof of what he meant is usually a *post hoc* analysis of a specific event after it has happened. Our perceptions of these events will change over time. They change as time cooks away the individual feelings surrounding them, and replaces them with what is then considered to be "a really true or more historically accurate" understanding. Of course those truths change over time as well, as they, too, are revisited and further "cooked" beyond all recognition.

What about significant events that occurred or that were actually observed by a single person?

Most scientists believe that singular observations are useless. However, what about the person who observes an event that alters his or her life forever. Good examples would be experiencing a vision at the fountain at Lourdes, perhaps healing cancer with the laying on of hands, or yes . . . being abducted from one's bed by small gray entities at four in the morning. I think you get my drift. Why do these events always have to have less meaning than when someone has been hit by a Mack truck? Don't they have just as much impact?

What about historical observations that have been made by thousands? We are left with a perception that somehow they are more valid because so many people were present. Unfortunately, those events become even more bogged down within history. Since they do affect so many of us and we are all personally connected in some way to a specific political, social, and theological agenda, such observations become quickly enmeshed or connected with these ideals. As our political, social, or theological agendas change, so do the constructs that, for a time, drove our beliefs.

History has a way of changing right along with our idealized beliefs, or vice versa. In some cases, this history making almost seems to take on a life of its own. The point is that the past, and events within it, are constantly modifying themselves to bring support to whatever the current political, social, or religious agenda might dictate.

One has only to look at almost any war, change in tribal or country boundary, or any significant movement within a culture or theology to see where an alteration of history or the record has taken place. Everyone is familiar with the phrase *"History is always written by the winners."*

The further we move away from the present and into the past, the more likely changes in that history have taken place, the more likely what we think we are seeing as real, isn't. On a scale of reality, it might look something like the graphic on the next page.

In my humble opinion, the past is a chameleon that always wears a tint of the "now." It fools us into thinking it is, or always was, an absolute, when, in fact, it has never been that way.

Someone once asked me, "What about the bones we dig up? Aren't they real?" Yes they are. But what defines the past is not so much the bones, but our perception of them, the context in which we display them.

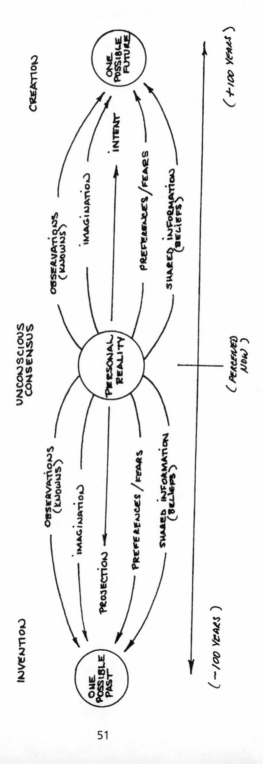

Historians wage a constant battle in trying to pin down reality. How they are being treated by the political, social, or religious pressures in the now of their time and place will usually dictate how they will report reality. While some are aware of this and strive to report it honestly, many don't. Since it is the political, social, and religious environment that pays for their work, endorses their findings, and passes judgment on them, who can blame them for doing otherwise? I simply suggest that we should always take what is *known* about the past with a large grain of salt. It's liable to morph itself right out from under our feet.

4

THE PRESENT

Show me any room, anywhere, with two, ten, or a hundred people in it, and I will show you two, ten, or a hundred different views of reality.

We all have different histories or backgrounds. We are all trained differently. Even those trained in the same field have different understandings of that field. We all carry different beliefs, and we are all in our own way prejudiced. In short, we all perceive things differently.

On the surface, we believe that everyone is pretty much in agreement with what reality means. Grass is green, the Earth revolves, gravity operates, fire burns, etc. This belief is born of what we share with one another. However, because our connection to reality is based on our sensorial input, we aren't in as much agreement as we would like to believe.

The way we process information dictates how we believe reality to be at any given moment. This is further modified by our perception of that great chameleon, the past, and how we personally relate to it. In fact, I believe that since our sensorial input requires processing, we never really exist in the present at all, but probably reside a shade away from the now. We actually are living within what could be called the most permanent expression of past that we can contemplate—that which is closest to our last moment of experience.

To demonstrate how this might work, we have only to look at our sense of sight. Even though we can smell, hear, touch, or taste something, most people (except the visually handicapped) will initially doubt the input from these senses if they can't see something. We seem to put a lot more confidence in our vision to tell us what is real or not real.

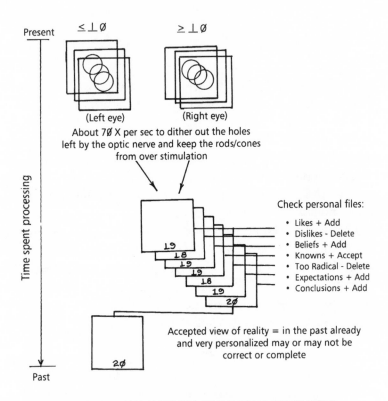

Present

≤ ⊥ Ø   ≥ ⊥ Ø

(Left eye)   (Right eye)

About 7Ø X per sec to dither out the holes
left by the optic nerve and keep the rods/cones
from over stimulation

Time spent processing

Check personal files:

- Likes + Add
- Dislikes - Delete
- Beliefs + Add
- Knowns + Accept
- Too Radical - Delete
- Expectations + Add
- Conclusions + Add

Accepted view of reality = in the past already
and very personalized may or may not be
correct or complete

Past

THE REAL WAY VISION PROBABLY OPERATES

As boring as it might be, most people don't understand even the most rudimentary issues surrounding sight, or how their vision works. Rather than go into a long-drawn-out technical description about vision, which you can find in any good encyclopedia, I will only briefly touch on it here.

To begin with, there are minute movements of the eyes that are irregular and of high frequency (30-70 per second). This occurs because if the light falling on the rods and cones remains in the same place for too long, the image being produced will disappear, a result of the retina adapting to the stimulus, which causes the messages being sent to the central nervous system to cease functioning.

We don't notice the constant movement since the brain is continually checking the position of the eyes in relation to the target and automatically correcting the errors in vision resulting from the movement. Vision is also suppressed during movement, otherwise our vision would be severely blurred.

So we are essentially seeing in snapshots, which are constantly being corrected for movement; movement that essentially suppresses vision.

I've always considered that to be one of the reasons UFOs are not seen by some people during major sighting events. The erratic or vibratory shifting of the UFO itself may coincide with the minimum/maximum rate at which the person's vision can adjust.

Most people believe that each eye is sending a picture in its entirety to one side of the brain or the other. In actuality, each eye is communicating with each side of the brain—right and left. Each side of the brain has an important but separate function with regard to cognition.

We also know that the eyes are further affected by light wavelength. Each eye transmits a perception of what the person is seeing to the brain. If both images are somewhat similar, it usually results in a stereoscopic appearance, but some data may be lost, depending on wavelength. As an example, if each eye looks through a different colored lens, the chromatic differences in magnification cause the images to be slightly different in size, creating a condition that might result in stereoscopic "illusion," as it becomes more difficult for the brain to decipher. It can sometimes fool the brain into thinking it is receiving a completely different picture, in which case the brain will usually discard one eye's input entirely, or in some cases, overlay one with the other, creating a third illusion.

What is apparent here, is that in a close-boundary or threshold dispute over what is being seen, the brain will make modifications it can live with. Translation: It will create a false picture.

Cognition, or the understanding of what we are seeing, is an even more complex issue. After the brain has decided what it is going to present as vision, we enter a processing mode that allows a higher order of cognition.

As an example, one of the first things we probably do is compare what we see with what we expected to see. This is based on our most recent past, perhaps the last pictogram we've recorded in memory. If there are major differences between these two perceptions, we will skip to the question of whether or not we are willing to accept those differences and what those differences might represent. Part of the acceptance of those differences is heavily impacted by our willingness or openness to change and our automatic bias and prejudice. Once we've decided that what we are seeing is acceptable, we acknowledge it as a clear and precise picture of reality, which we always refer to as "now."

The problem is, depending on the cognitive processes and how much time it takes, we are now somewhere in the past and no longer in the now.

What is most interesting, is that our assumed present would probably be more accurately described as a past based on the past. In other words, change, at least as it is pertinent to our perception of reality, is a very slow process, heavily modified and severely controlled by us. What we perceive as the present, cannot exist without its connection to the past—a past that isn't as fixed as we might believe or desire it to be, and one of our own creation.

When we begin to venture into the idea of a future, the situation becomes even more complex.

As this is a book about the future, the future is addressed more completely in a following chapter. At this point, it is only necessary to understand that our future is more than likely a result of actions we are taking in a perceived or personal now.

Because these actions are always based on our perceptions of reality as gleaned from our inventive "now" and modified by our beliefs relevant to the past (which, due to political, social, or theological events, may be changing), it is no longer in dispute that past, present, and future, are inexorably tied together in some holistic way. All are mobile, one affecting the other. Reality probably looks more like a constantly stirred soup, with the past, present, and future being mixed together—all residing within our own pot!

5

HISTORICAL VIEWING

To understand what remote viewing the future is all about, we have to have a clear idea of the kind of political and social pressures that exist around remote viewing itself. None bring these more quickly to the surface than remote viewing the past and publishing the results.

We live in a world filled with mystery, especially about our past. Remote viewing can bring a lot of the past into the light of day. By targeting these mysteries, producing information relative to them, then publishing or opening up access to this information, one voluntarily opens to doing battle on many fronts.

Even when there is a lack of hard evidence to argue or stand up against the remote viewing data, someone will come forward to attack it, simply because of its source.

Historians, anthropologists, archaeologists, or theologians will most frequently generate negative comments. Their comments are usually based on their experience with other subjects, or they may stem purely from their viewpoints or beliefs regarding the paranormal.

Where remote viewing may support some of their viewpoints or beliefs, one can expect either no comment, or an "I told you so." Where there is disagreement, however, you can count on an attack on all fronts.

To illustrate this, I will give an example of a target in the past that I remote viewed back in 1980. It's a good example, since I can now provide evidence that most of what I said at the time was eventually proven correct.

Surprise Example

I was working a series of remote viewings that were intended to evaluate a remote viewer's capability of distinguishing between one kind of technology and another. The pool (a collection of targets), by necessity, was constructed of what were considered to be "higher technology targets." Of course, the pool, as well as its contents, was kept blind to me as the remote viewer. Targets selected from this randomized pool included such things as a deep-fat frying machine, a computer mother-board, an aircraft engine, a weather satellite, the inner workings of a ballpoint pen, etc. The exercise was designed to determine the quality and depth of detail that could be achieved through remote viewing.

To regress a bit, most who have worked at studying the paranormal within a lab environment know that after a while, when a psychic or remote viewer has been repeatedly tasked with somewhat similar targets, or a lot of targets, in a repetitive fashion—aside from fighting off the obvious overlay problems that begin to encroach on the mind of the viewer—boredom with lab work begins to set in.

Boredom will inevitably produce a slow but sure slide backward to what might be considered a "normal" condition. That is, a condition that for a remote viewer translates to mean no psychic functioning is taking place. Since I usually do a number of targets in an experiment, we tried something new to reduce or eliminate the boredom factor.

They decided that somewhere within any series of targets, in this case twelve, they would insert an extra (thirteenth) target that would be completely different from all of the rest. Because I was told there would be a radically different target somewhere in the pile, it was hoped that this would keep me interested and focused. No one knew when this target would come up, because it was inserted within the series, which was being selected from randomly. So the wild card could have been the first target I was to work, the fifth, the eleventh, or the last. Providence would provide.

I want to point out that although the twelve targets were technology targets of varying degrees, I was not privy to that information at the time. The expectation or reason for targeting that I was given before each remote viewing was simply "We are looking for as much detail as possible on these targets."

I can't recall when the radically different target came up, but I do remember that it occurred in the second half of the thirteen-target series, perhaps seventh or eighth.

The individual targets were usually pictures with the names of specific machines, each placed within a larger, double-wrapped and opaque envelope, not unlike the large manila envelopes you will find at any office supply. I was not allowed to handle the envelopes, but they were placed on a table in the room in which I was doing the remote viewing. All envelopes were identified with numbers randomly chosen at the time they were placed in the pool. The person who chose the random numbers was not the person who had selected the targets, so there was no way to know in which order they would appear.

At the beginning of the session for the mystery target, I was asked to provide as much detail as I could, the same requirement as with all those that preceded it. By then, I had developed a "feel" for the pool, which means I knew it would probably pertain to some kind of technology. What technology, I couldn't say. In a sense this created a form of overlay, which was also creating a great deal of difficulty for me at the time.

After a cool-down period of about half an hour, I *opened* to the target and got my first impressions, which surprised the monitor almost as much as it surprised me.

My first impression was of a very large and placid lake—a lake just before sunrise. The surface was light blue and very smooth, barely a perceived ripple. It was fed from the south by a large river, moving swiftly, but also smooth. Water exited the lake to the north also by a river, but in the latter case, it had been partially dammed, helping to create a much larger lake than would normally have been there. A jungle of green foliage, giving a sense of a tropical or near-tropical climate surrounded the lake. The jungle was lush, green, and abundant—filled with food.

Within the lake, somewhere near the edge, I perceived two very large rafts. These were lashed firmly in place and facing one another. Other, slightly smaller, rafts were traveling toward or away from these two larger rafts, and appeared to be in some kind of a procession. I had a sense they were all somehow being used for the same thing. Stacked across the center of both the larger rafts were huge blocks of stone. Each stone was cut perfectly smooth on five sides, with the sixth side left somewhat rough. One very large block was actually being lowered into the water with a swing type of crane, sort of an A-frame on the front of the raft. Ropes from the second raft were guiding the stone.

Beside the rafts were men who appeared to be walking on the surface of the smooth water. Some of them were bending over or crouched on their knees, and some had tools in their hands. All a very curious display.

Of course my monitor, who was also blind to whatever target I was working on, was quite intrigued by all this. Men walking on water? Rafts sinking large blocks of stone into a lake? None of it seemed to make any sense.

And of course, the gist of the information differed radically from any previous information I had been giving on the earlier targets.

The monitor suggested that I might want to collect my thoughts and readdress the target. I tried very hard to blank my mind and do what he suggested.

My second attempt at this particular target only added more mystery to the session. I followed the departing rafts as they slowly moved against the slight current within the lake, toward a place somewhere in the south. There, a few kilometers from the base of some cliffs, was a formal docking area, constructed also of large cut blocks of stone that had been carefully interlocked. Two piers jutted outward into the lake, each being only inches above the water line. I reported that the source of the stones apparently was these clifflike areas, where they were being cut and shaped using somewhat primitive tools.

The stones, once prepared, were then placed on sleds that were moved down a formal road to the docks. This road was also constructed from large segments of stone, cut into thick layers, then paved with some kind of hardened material, not unlike a smooth, hard-baked clay finish.

It appeared that every way in which water could be used to assist or aid in the work, it was being used.

The surface of the lake itself was being used as a near-perfect reference plane for the large pad of stones being laid just below its surface. Once lowered into the water, the stones were being carefully and deliberately shaved to within fractions of an inch of level, using the plane of water as a guide. The first two or three courses of stone thus being laid perfectly flat, fitted exactly, and with great precision. Water lubricated the saws, which were made of soft metal and which otherwise would not have worked.

Large fires and heat were being used against the cliff face to prepare great portions of rock for removal. Once heated in narrow channels, the rock was being doused with the cold water from the lake, forming cracks into which more heat could be placed. The rock was doused again, reheated, then doused again, eventually creating larger and larger cracks, until huge slabs of stone sheared away from the cliff face, falling into a work area where the pieces were then being sized and squared. Again, using water as a lubricant, large soaking pits contained segments of stone yet to be worked. The water apparently had some softening effect on the stone, making it more malleable to the types of primitive tools being used. The tools included water-lubricated saws and small flat chisels, made of a soft alloy or cast metal. Not ideal for working stone, but given the type of stone, the use of water and soaking, good enough to get the job done.

Once sized, the large stones were jacked up on one side and a sled was constructed piecemeal beneath them—first one side then the other. Once the sled was finished, the stones were moved along the smooth paved road to the waiting rafts. Again water was used, this time to lubricate the roadway, which was constructed at an angle and fell toward the lake.

Following a suggestion from the monitor to move forward in time (an interesting perception—targeting the future in the past), I noticed some interesting cycles occurring within the lake. Its size and depth were increasing over time. This controlled flooding was being accomplished with the annual addition of more stone to the dam, the same kinds of stones being used at the primary construction site. A narrow neck of the river was selected for the construction of the dam.

As the water level rose, so did the levels of construction, both at the primary site as well as the dam site.

It is difficult to say the period of time involved in the construction at the primary site. Sense of time or its accuracy varies greatly among remote viewers. Some are good at it; some are not. Being prodded by the monitor for an estimate of how long this construction might have gone on, I remember saying that it probably did not exceed a lifetime. My guess would be fifty years.

Trying to pin down how long ago the construction might have taken place is a whole different story. Nothing about the dress, tools, rafts, or people matched anything I remember from my history books. My sense is that what I was witnessing was being accomplished by a race of people who vanished long before our earliest recorded history. These people probably existed at the very least fifteen to twenty thousand years ago.

We terminated the remote viewing session as mystified as we had been when we started. Turning in the materials, the monitor and I asked for feedback on the target. Inside the envelope was the following:

"Describe how the Great Pyramid of Giza was constructed."

Fascinated with the possibilities, on a later trip to SRI-International, I attempted to turn over the information to their Egyptology lab, and was laughed out of the room. Such information simply flies in the face of common belief (at least it did so back then). I was told there was not a scintilla of evidence that would support any of the information I had produced.

Talk about no feedback. In 1980, there was no one who would entertain even a notion that there might be something of value contained within my remote viewing. Having no feedback, it could only be considered "science fiction." While it may have been of great interest to me or to my monitor, it had no value outside simply being "interesting." As much as I might not like it, I had to agree, and simply filed it away as fun but useless.

Let's now look at what could have been done with this information. I've always said that even if a remote viewing can't be verified, it may still be worth a closer look. If it were simply used to target or direct other information-collection systems, it would have value. In this case, archaeologists, anthropologists, geologists, or engineers could have gotten a leg up on their peers had they simply been open enough to the possibilities.

Based on the information from this remote viewing, an insightful geologist could have computed the expected location of the lakeshore, consistent with the depth of flooding required to build the lower layers of the pyramid. That would have given a possible location for the docks and ramps that were used to load the rafts. Certainly finding such docks or ramps would be a strong indication that some of the other remote viewing information might have also been correct.

The molecular content of deposits between the stones, obtained through core sampling, particularly at the lower levels of the pyramid, might show signs of those stones having being submerged for an extended period of time.

It may be that a lake large enough or deep enough to build the great pyramid was then, and is now, beyond the capacity of man. However, the remote viewing provides a strong link to the possibility that the stones were at least transported by water. Perhaps, too, a shallow version of the dammed lake described within the remote viewing might have been sufficient to lay in the first two or three layers of base stone, ensuring the nearly impossible task of beginning with a near-perfect foundation plane.

My current understanding of the level of difficulty regarding the construction of the pyramid, at least from an engineering standpoint, is the near impossibility of achieving a perfectly flat and balanced plane in the first few courses of stone. Attempts at replicating pyramid construction using modern construction techniques and equipment have essentially failed because of an inability to produce this very exact and near perfect plane of reference at the base. If one doesn't begin with a near-perfect base, the difference in weight from corner to corner when combined with gravity tends to cause a pyramid to self-destruct long before it is finished.

Using rafts to transport the stones in a land where heavy wheels were usually replaced with sleds for moving extremely large objects makes perfect sense.

Projections could have been made of what the Nile Delta might have looked like fifteen thousand years ago. There might not have even been a delta per se during that specific time period. Owing to the fact that a lush and tropical jungle was perceived as circling the lake, both the river and its effluence into the Mediterranean Basin area could have been entirely different at that time. There might not have been a Mediterranean Sea as we now know it, but instead mighty waterfalls.

The area surrounding the Great Pyramid, which is now arid and dry, most certainly has an effect on how the Nile appears to us today. It has everything to do with its flow, rate of surge, and the creation of the great Nile Delta that now exists north of Cairo. One would have to believe that such an arid place would have to have developed rather rapidly to have gone from near Congo-type jungle to desert in so short a period as 15,000 years. But there are currently other areas on our planet that are changing to desert in an even more rapid fashion, so this is not an impossibility. Such changes are usually due to a rapid or sudden change in the local ecosystem. Recent core samples from the deepest portions of the Mediterranean show the upper portions of the cores to contain nearly pure salt. This would imply that at some time in the past the Mediterranean Basin was probably dry. In other words, the Mediterranean Sea didn't exist. Perhaps the gateway to the ocean at Gibraltar was sealed fifteen to twenty thousand years ago, and the bulk of humanity (world population at the time) resided where the sea is today. Brings a whole new perspective to the idea of Noah's Flood, doesn't it?

In any event, the sudden flooding of the Mediterranean Basin would have had a major impact on the ecological balance in the area, especially when combined with prevailing winds.

But . . . I forget. I'm obviously getting too far out in front of myself. While this is all fascinating stuff, without appropriate feedback, it will have to remain science fiction.

Or does it?

Feedback

I can now provide an answer to my viewing in 1980, by referring to an article that was published in the *Los Angeles Times* on Saturday, May 7, 1994:

> American researchers have discovered what they say is the world's oldest paved road: a 4,600-year-old highway that linked a basalt quarry in a desolate, deserted region of the Egyptian desert to waterways that carried basalt blocks to monument sites along the Nile.
> The eight-mile-long road is at least 500 years older than any previously discovered road and is the only paved road discovered in ancient Egypt, said geologist Thomas Bown of the U.S. Geological Survey in Denver, who will report the discovery Friday at a regional meeting of the Geological Society of America in Durango, Colorado. *The road probably doesn't rank with the pyramids as a construction feat, but it is a major engineering achievement,* said his colleague, geologist James Harrell of the University of Toledo in Ohio. *Not only is the road earlier than we thought possible, we didn't even think they built roads.*
> The researchers made an additional discovery in the quarry at the northern end of the road, the first evidence that the Egyptians used rock saws for cutting the basalt into blocks. *This is the oldest example of saws being used for cutting stone,* said archaeologist James K. Hoffmeier of Wheaton College in Illinois. *That's two technologies we didn't know they had,* Harrell said in a telephone interview. *And we don't know why they were both abandoned.*
> The road was discovered in the Faiyum Depression, a low area about 45 miles southwest of Cairo. Short segments of the road had been observed by earlier explorers of the area, Bown said, but they failed to realize its significance or to follow up on their observations. Bown and his

colleagues stumbled across it accidentally while they were doing geological mapping in the region.

The road was clearly built to serve the newly discovered quarry, where the heavy black basalt was laid down by volcanic eruptions about 30 million years ago. Bown and Harrell have found the camp that housed the workers at the quarry, and numerous pottery shards and artifacts date the site to the Egyptian 'Old Kingdom,' which began about 2600 B.C.

The road appears today to go nowhere, ending in the middle of the parched desert. When it was built, however, its terminus was a quay on the shore of Lake Moeris, which had an elevation of about 66 feet above sea level, the same as the quay. Birket Qarun, the lake that is now at the bottom of the depression, has a surface elevation of 148 feet below sea level, reflecting the sharp change in climate in the region.

Lake Moeris received its water from the annual floods of the Nile River. At the time of the floods, the river and lake were at the same level and connected through a gap in the hills near the modern villages of el-Lahun and Hawara. Harrell and Bown believe basalt blocks were loaded onto barges during the dry season, then floated over to the Nile during the floods to be shipped off to the monument sites at Giza and Saqqara.

The road was constructed with flagstones, large slabs of stone that were laid on the sand without any surface preparation. The nature of the stones varies according to location on the road. *It's clear they just used whatever was handy,* Bown said.

The road is a little over six feet wide—*almost exactly four cubits,* Bown said. Although the main road is just under eight miles long, branches at the quarry bring the total to about 11 miles."

Suddenly the remote viewing doesn't read so much like science fiction any longer.

I actually began talking about this remote viewing with participants in Gateway Programs, at The Monroe Institute, as early as 1985. I shared some of this remote viewing with hundreds of people, primarily to show that while remote viewing history may make for fascinating copy, there is really very little one can do to get someone to accept it as real information.

In this case, I waited seventeen years for feedback that partially validates what I was perceiving back in 1980.

Again, I reiterate, the accuracy of remote viewing is seldom 100 percent. In this example, there is still a lot unknown about the target. But I believe there will be more data coming in relative to this remote viewing. Perhaps within my lifetime I will know that I was right about how the Great Pyramid was constructed.

The Kennedy Assassination

Rather than go into a long and complex venue, describing word for word, or item by item, my perceptions regarding the assassination of John F. Kennedy, I can sum up these perceptions quite succinctly by specifically addressing who, how, and why.

1. Who?

Ultimately this question leads to Cuba and the motive. If one insists on trying to blame a single element of the government, the Mafia, enemies of America, or a lone gunman, there is no answer. Also, if one insists on creating a very large, complex, and extensive conspiracy to carry the blame, this will also lead to a dead end.

In reality, it was part or a portion of both. A conspiracy—certainly—but a small one. One based on a single string of connections that ran from the top down. A line of interest within which all the participants viewed their actions as being patriotic, but for different reasons.

To understand where it all began, one would have to go back to the Cuban Missile Crisis. As Americans, our perception of this event is heavily tainted with our national pride and emotion. When viewed under a bright light however, what we find is this:

A less-than-popular president, faced with a direct Soviet threat, chose to go toe-to-toe with a less-than-sophisticated student of Stalin. If and when all the classified material relevant to this event is finally released, we will see a situation that was probably the most dangerous ever faced by humanity (never mind America or Russia.) We probably came about as close to thermonuclear war as one would ever want to come in any form of crisis. I strongly believe that there were at least a handful of men within the upper echelon of our government that viewed this as primarily Kennedy's fault, or at a minimum, badly handled by him.

Whether true or not, as a result, there was a very real belief (at least within their minds) that there was a strong possibility for such an event occurring again at some future date.

If so, what do you do?

You now suddenly have a very popular president, both politically (on the inside) as well as publicly (on the outside). And . . . God forbid . . . as a result, an improved probability for another confrontation—one no one will walk away from.

Radically concerned with the welfare and survival of their nation, and with their ability for action severely restricted, I can see where the idea of assassination would become a possible alternative.

2. How?

Having made up your mind to take such a despicable action, how do you do it? You need someone who is willing to take the risk, do the job. Certainly, at that level of government, you aren't going to do the job yourself. In this case, we have a lot to select from.

Cuban Expatriates.

There are a lot of people who say that the newly arriving Cuban refugees to America were general supporters of Kennedy. This is true, but only in the sense that they saw him as their only hope to return to their homeland. After the Bay of Pigs fiasco, there was no doubt on the streets of Miami how most of the Cuban Freedom Fighters felt about JFK. One might be able to argue a case that a majority of the refugee population eventually realized that, both politically and reasonably, taking back Cuba by force was not an appropriate solution. However, for sake of our argument, it only requires a few people within a loosely knit organizational structure to provide necessary support to an assassination. The bonus is that they are probably already trained militarily, as well as in the arts of clandestine operations.

Organized Crime.

In my lifetime, I've met members of organized crime. Most of them would die before they would allow something to happen to the president of the United States. However, having said that, I must also say that those who might have had their "business" interfered with are not so patriotic.

During World War II, there were a number of noted organized crime figures who participated in our efforts against the Nazi or Japanese war machines. Make no mistake, they did this because it was good for business. They scratched our government's back; we scratched theirs.

A couple of notable crime families were dealt heavy blows by Castro's nationalizing of casinos in Havana. The damage might have been repaired if the United States government had backed off in some of its policies toward Cuba. However, JFK was instrumental in pursuing policies that guaranteed the door to Cuba would be slammed shut for good. This was a crime against "business," and one that any member of those families would have jumped at reconciling.

I believe the organization, manning, coordination, and execution of JFK's assassination was engineered and carried out by at least one of those crime families, in conjunction with at least one of the Cuban expatriate organizations that existed at that time.

They provided the equipment, which included at a minimum transportation, guns, money, safe houses, and protection for at least four shooters. They also provided a plan and the patsy—one Lee Harvey Oswald.

While there may have been some rogue contract agents working as interface between the Central Intelligence Agency and the Cuban/organized crime groups that were directly involved, I do not believe any badge-carrying member of the CIA, FBI, or Secret Service was privy to the operation.

I do believe the originators/initiators of the plan came from at least the cabinet level of the government, and they probably used less than a handful of resources within their offices (DoD) to effect coordination between them and the Cuban/organized crime organizations concerned.

When JFK was shot, he was fired on from at least three (possibly four) positions. The bullet that killed him struck him from the front, and was fired through a street-level storm drain—hence the perception that the rifle fire was coming from all directions. In actuality, that was the only rifle that did not have a silencer on it, because of the range from which it was being fired.

3. Why?

There has been quite a lot of speculation that Kennedy was shot to prevent him from giving a speech in Dallas where he would be talking about unidentified flying objects and aliens. I don't believe this to be true. The kind of planning necessary to carry out his assassination required many more months of planning than would have been possible following the writing of his speech.

There are also those who think the plot runs deeper and wider than I may be outlining here, but I doubt that it does.

I do not think that Vice President Johnson was in any way implicated in the plot because of Vietnam or any other political situation ongoing at the time. In subsequent historical viewings that revolved around President Johnson, I have always gotten a sense that this man was genuinely disturbed by the whole issue of Vietnam and carried these issues and the decisions he was forced to make regarding the policies there with a great deal of personal pain and hidden anguish. I think Johnson regretted every American life lost in Vietnam. Unfortunately, he was associated in part with people who chose not to take any personal responsibility for their thoughts, recommendations, or actions.

There are also rumors that JFK had planned to announce the breaking up and dissolution of the Central Intelligence Agency. Even if this were so, it would not have been a reason to kill him. The jobs that were being carried out by the CIA at the time would have simply shifted to new agencies and carried on where they had left off.

As an example, the Defense Intelligence Agency (DIA) was established on August 21, 1961, in reaction to the missile gap "crisis" of the late 1950s. One of thirteen Department of Defense (DoD) agencies, its primary job is to perform counterintelligence in support of the Joint Chiefs of Staff, supervise the DoD Indications and Warning System, and manage the General Defense Intelligence Program, the Defense Attaché System, Target Data Inventory for the DoD, and contribute to the NIE & NFIB,(National Intelligence Estimates/Special National Intelligence Estimates Board, and is a member of the National Foreign Intelligence Board.) In conjunction with the National Security Agency (NSA), the two agencies probably control about 98 percent of the defense reconnaissance taking place across the world.

I think the CIA and its personnel, while officially ceasing to exist, would have simply been absorbed into one of these major agencies. Back then (1962), very few people even knew that the National Security Agency/Central Security

Service (NSA/CSS) existed. In 1990, the last reliable figures I have within my files indicate that NSA/CSS had an estimated personnel strength of twenty to twenty-four thousand, and an annual budget of over three billion dollars; this does not include support from the Army, Air Force, and Navy. The Army support alone in 1990 constituted approximately 120 thousand personnel in 183 installations across the world.

In fact, anyone generating any effort within any of the defense or intelligence agencies that included the planned assassination of an American president would have been vulnerable to the very institution for which they would have been working. While not all systems are perfect, I seriously doubt that they could have hidden such operations completely, or prevented them from eventually being discovered. One might postulate that were such a covert operation uncovered in the future, every effort would be made to bury it by the controlling agency. I believe just the opposite would occur. Uncovering the full details behind the assassination of an American president would probably be the single greatest intelligence coup in the history of intelligence. Not something anyone would want to see buried, for obvious political and personal reasons.

So why was he killed? He was killed by a handful of people whose sole intention was to prevent what they believed would be an eventual war to end all wars—and the thermonuclear destruction of the planet. Their plan was engineered and carried out by players who had their own, more personal motivations, most of which were probably not political.

Could Kennedy's assassination have been prevented?

Possibly, but given the attitude of the time, I doubt it. I think he was killed because of the kind of man he was. He had a very firm grasp on and understanding of the political use of power, probably something he learned at a very early age from his father. That political savvy, mixed with his persona, projected a volatile and threatening personality to some of the men who felt they had been tasked with a higher responsibility to the country—albeit a twisted one.

Contrary to these men's fears, had John F. Kennedy lived, I think we would have seen a very different world by the early 1970s—one in which the doctrine of reciprocal deterrence, or Mutual Assured Destruction, could not have operated or survived. Now we will never know.

6

OTHER HISTORICAL EXPLORATIONS

During an extended period of experimentation at the Monroe Institute, in Faber, Virginia, in 1983, I did a number of "explorer sessions" with Robert Monroe, the author of *Journeys Out of the Body*, 1971; *Far Journeys*, 1985; and *Ultimate Journey*, 1994, Doubleday and Company.

These explorer sessions were not based on a remote viewing protocol, but were performed exactly as titled. Bob would take a subject into his lab and hook them up to biomonitoring equipment. He would then subject them to varying mixes of Hemi-Sync signals[1] to achieve a form of altered-state perception. Once he could see that the subject was in an altered state, he would then ask a question. The question was usually worded to disguise the actual intent of his experiment, or in some way mask what he was actually after.

Under a great deal of pressure from my friends, I've decided to share two of the explorer sessions in which I was a participant. I'm doing this for a number of reasons. I want to show just how far back one can journey into time, and how interesting the responses can be—especially when relatively blind. I would caution the reader to understand that neither Bob Monroe, nor anyone else, actually knows where the information may originate. In all of the years of research he did, no clear proof was ever produced that guarantees where the information comes from. On the other hand, there were many of what one could call "very good clues." Over the years, Bob came to feel very strongly that the information was probably originating from some kind of a holistic or general "information field." I tend to agree with him.

In the simplest of terms, I believe that all knowledge exists in a pure form. For lack of a better word, I will call it "spiritual." David Bohm, Ph.D. refers to this state of matter as the "implicate order," the physical being the "explicate order." For Hindus it's the "Brahman." This is a general concept that is also supported by kabalistic commentary, numerous other religions, as well as nearly all forms of shamanistic teachings. In other words, all things in reality just exist, and are therefore accessible.

Using the modern techniques of Hemi-Sync, Bob Monroe was able to engineer a direct contact between us normal human beings and this knowledge bank, vis-à-vis a deeper altered state. The following is the first example of such an explorer session.

The Jesus Transcript

This session was taped in the Monroe Institute laboratory on December 28, 1983. The actual targeting material was contained within a double-wrapped, opaque envelope, with the following question written on a piece of folded paper inside:

"Who or what was Jesus, and why was he here?"

I was asked to go to my remote viewing window—a place commonly referred to back then as "The Library." Once there, I was asked to tell the monitor when I was ready. The monitor was Robert A. Monroe, and there were no other personnel within the lab during the session. The session lasted seventy-eight minutes, including pauses, some which exceeded five minutes in length. Robert Monroe of course knew what the question in the envelope was. As monitor, he was in a room remote from the isolation chamber that I was lying in.

This isolation chamber is a large black cube, heavily soundproofed, and fully shielded with copper sheeting. It is engineered to dampen vibrations other than what might be felt as a result of the Hemi-Sync process.

Once I was relaxed within this cube, Bob would throw a switch to his microphone when he wished to speak to me, otherwise, I was speaking into a mike that was recording my responses.

Because we were remote from one another, and the isolation cube was dark, the possibility of Monroe leading me with body language was eliminated. However, there is still cause for concern that he was leading me by the way he phrased his questions. I will leave it to the reader to decide.

After a long pause of nine minutes, in which I was adjusting to the changes in Hemi-Sync signals he was piping into the booth, I told him that I was ready.

Joe: OK. Whenever.

Bob: Now that you are at the library, tell us something about the target in the envelope.

Joe: Something seems to be very active here. This really seems to be very interesting . . . I have a sense of some kind of energy forms which are coming and going. I've not seen them before today.

Bob: Tell us something about them.

Joe: There is a next level in here which I wasn't perceiving as well before. I'm perceiving an exterior to this place which has an airplane-like appearance without wings. It's sitting on a flat rock of a place in the middle of what appears to be a large cavern, or cave, or something. (I'm describing the library here.)

Bob: Is your library . . . is this a vehicle of some kind?

Joe: Apparently it is . . . the library itself is a vehicle of some kind . . . and the exterior appears to be a physical thing. However, the interior seems to be more of a sensed kind of thing—more esoteric kind of thing—not real, but real. When you're inside of it, it appears to be extremely large. When you're outside, it appears to be very small . . . you know, large, but not as large as it appears on the inside.

Bob: Why don't you move around inside, explore the inside, see what develops in reference to the target envelope, which I now have in my shirt pocket.

Joe: OK.

Bob: Your target is important, specifically because of its impact on our civilization, so see what information you can search out in reference to the target.

Joe: Ok. I see a tube . . . a tube of light. I'm going to try and interface with it. It's an energy column or beam or whatever they would call it.

Bob: An energy beam?

Joe: Yes. That's what it appears to be. I don't remember ever seeing anything like this here before. It might have something to do with the target.

Bob: Interface with it then and tell me what you feel.

Joe: Just a minute. (long pause)

Joe: I'm getting an impression of a very interesting Being. Ah . . . getting a . . . getting like an advanced Being here that is . . . ah . . . temporarily occupied the body of a man named . . . (chuckle) . . . named Jesus.

My laugh was a direct result of humor passed to me by this being that I was sensing—almost a jovial, fun type of feeling.

Apparently this Being was ah . . . ah . . . this is really fascinating, it's like a double loop kind of thing. The . . . this man called Jesus was a multiple aspect . . . evidently . . . personality? One of his higher selves took control of the physical . . . the physical body, for some reason. I'm trying not to create overlay here. I'm trying to find the reason. Evidently there is a . . . (long pause)

During this very long pause, Bob thought that I had actually gone to sleep, which frequently happened when he "unreeled" to such a deep altered state at the edge of consciousness.

Bob: It's OK, you can continue with what you were saying.

Joe: . . . it has to do with the salvation of an ideal. There were too many ideals, so there was required a consolidation of ideals. Ah . . . it's also very interesting, in that . . . this wasn't the first time this happened.

(another long pause)

Joe: . . . hope this is Jesus you're interested in. I think this is so. (pause) Where was I? (pause) It's like on a number of occasions . . . one of the occasions was the . . . time just before the period of Greece . . . the Grecians.

The frequency of pauses is usually a result of mental detachment. The dissassociation or detachment was one of the effects resulting from the type of Hemi-Sync mix that Bob usually used with the explorers. This was varied based on the biofeedback he was seeing on his monitors during the session in real time. As someone who had experienced this many times, it was somewhat akin to being at the very edge of sleep, where one is totally detached from one's sense of being. It was certainly very difficult staying awake and concentrating on what was actually going on. In some cases, I would retain no memory of what was said at all.

Bob: Tell me something about that.

Joe: Primitive man . . . yes . . . primitive man knows of this in the South Americas. There was a time when ah . . . a speaker, or teacher walked among two or three Indian tribes in the Americas.

Bob: Is that the only time?

Joe: In a physical sense only for a short while did this happen . . . ah . . . less than ten years, and then he vanished. There was a time in the beginning of Grecian history that it happened again. It was prior to the Greek philosophers. There were two or three places of learning established. There was also a time in the . . . ah . . . in China. There was a learned man who walked there. I have a strong sense of commonality in this, incidentally. They were all cases of a physical manifestation of . . . where the physical manifestation was all somewhat similar. A tall man, six foot two, or six foot three, abnormally large for that period of time. Ah . . . auburn hair, light skinned, no olive tint to skin, in all cases, it was an abnormal physical manifestation of this energy . . . this Being, this aspect of Being—a truly powerful human being.

Bob: Tell us something about the importance of this Being you are calling Jesus. Tell us something about the more important years of this Being.

Joe: Oh . . . that would have been later, at least . . . feels like later.

(long pause)

Joe: This man I call Jesus was crazy. Not crazy as we understand the term, totally crazy for his times . . . I guess. His culture would have called him crazy. And ah . . . he was seeking a form of truth. Apparently, there is truth to his going into the desert when in early . . . in his early twenties. There he stayed with a tribe of people. I get the . . . I just get like a group of people that were culturally different, in a significant way. Ah . . . almost one-eighty out of phase with the rest of the existent world at the time . . . or at least the world this man came from. I see a tremendous amount of physical sacrifice and meditation, an attempt to grasp the truth, and . . . ah . . . attempt to sheer away from the politics of the time, the indulgences of the time. There, he allowed this aspect to take control of him . . . a powerful occurrence, which caused some differences even in his physical manifestation. Then ah . . . . he came to where or what was then the center of learning for an entire race of people who were strong enough to remain separate, to be different.

(long pause—probably off getting information)

Joe: What I find interesting here is the . . . apparently there was a knowing or a knowledgeability that this teacher had . . . of the . . . ah . . . the frug . . . ah . . . ah . . . oh hell, how in the heck am I going to translate this? Bear with me for a moment . . . the necessity to mask the ideal. And ah . . . so he chose an esoteric, or a mystification that was different from all the others that was . . . er, were existent. All the others . . . the other mystifications were dependent on physical reward. And these ideals (of his) were masked in a lack of need for physical reward. It had an interesting effect, in that it seemed to spark something within the intellect of man.

Bob: Move forward in time and tell us something about this Being's primary objective.

Joe: OK. Hold on for a moment.

(long pause)

Joe: Hmmmmmmm. There is an answer here . . . It's kind of neat. It's not like knowledge you would expect. It's more like a . . . the ideal is that . . . in his ideal it is important to understand that in the interaction of the elements, all the elements of the whole, we would call that human race by the way, there is ah . . . the interaction itself is the learning, the development, the growth of mankind. And that in that interaction, that growth, between people . . . apparently the static on the line or the interference in the process is created by what we call fear. I'm looking for a reason for fear.

(long pause)

Joe: And . . . ah . . . the answer that I am getting is . . . when we reach a certain point of understanding and learning we don't need it anymore. The whole idea was to establish that there was fear. His ideal is to make us understand there is fear and how to . . . deal with it, learn to deal with it. That fear is nothing—our own creation. And that ah . . . the opposites of fear are within the focus of life. Some would call that love of fellow man, but this is not true. It is far more encompassing than that. It's the drive to interact. Human beings must interact, we are driven to it, in order to learn. There is no set piece of truth. As in the interaction between human beings, neither . . . of any side can claim truth. It's the interaction that's important. It's like where neither . . . of any two sides can claim perfection within an argument. It's like truth is a result of a pure form of interaction—but without fear. It's what creates truth. Then all sides can see clearly. Such a truth, a truth evolving out of interaction, does in itself then interact with other truths, which develop into a even further reaching out of truth—a more encompassing truth. It's a growth in simpler terms, like a tree growing. Constructed of all elements, none specifically good or bad. In order to get rid of the fear and do that however, the specific fear has to be identified.

(long pause)

Joe: In the case of this manifestation, this man I'm calling Christ, it was to show that there was no such thing as fear . . . other than as a self-imposed creation. But . . . he did all of this in a very mystical way, though. It originally wasn't meant to be. I sense history played a hand in the overmystification of the message. People quickly lost sight of the reasons for what happened because of the remystification. The ideals are the same, however, we are always wanting to go back and understand the ideals as they were then, but the basic ideals are the same, they don't change.

Bob: Tell us something about the immediate effect of his teachings. Was there something that we have missed?

Joe: That's an interesting question, which I don't know. I'll try and find out . . . give me a moment . . . to . . . ah . . .

(long pause)

Joe: The ah . . . (chuckle) . . . the life as chronicled, is inaccurate.

Bob: How?

Joe: There was an awful lot left out. There was very little data passed through the . . . ah . . . through the . . . what was then perceived as a secret brotherhood. Bits and pieces were sewn together in a pattern and embellished, hashed over, talked about, edited, edited, etc. The man was far more intense, far more ah . . . ah . . . what do you say? Far more . . . ah . . . nonparticipating in what was going on around him. It was as if he knew the course, so to speak, but knew the result, and . . . ah . . . pursued it with a very intense way about him. It doesn't appear that the intensity is established in any way, historically that is. Ah . . . he had another interesting thing here . . . he had a tremendous understanding of communications with people in his time. He understood the more . . . ah . . . it was like a building scale of things, the faster he climbed the scale of communications with the people, the more effectiveness he would have. I need to clarify this. It's kind of like . . . ah . . . an allegory today would be, to start by writing to a local newspaper and then wind up syndicated in seventy-five newspapers, fifty television stations, etc. He did this kind of communicating in a period of six years . . . We're talking phenomenal growth. He understood this . . . this patterning of lines, orchestrating and developing this form of interaction. He was the cause of people discussing it . . . the ideal . . . whether they agreed with it or not. He forced them to do this.

(long pause)

Joe: There seems like there is a missing piece here too, and I'm trying to grasp it. Hold on a second. Let me . . .

(long pause)

Joe: He ah . . . he was very ah . . . evidently he had a far greater deal of . . . a far greater number of people followed him as opposed to what's known or available in the historical record. He ah . . . he didn't spend time detailing his ideals or anything to like . . . student type of people. But, he did take the more brilliant people he became involved with and ah . . . and instructed them in the philosophic side of the ideal. He secretly made them understand the necessity for the interaction. They in turn, with that single key, spread their information as well. It was as if it was all hinged on a single precept. I think the historical record is a compilation of not only information from this man I call Jesus, but . . . an awful lot of information was credited to him that was provided by or taught by others based on a like premise, and included as well.

Bob: How about the end of his life? Can you provide any information that might be relevant?

Joe: I want to say . . . the death was as represented . . . but he didn't die on a cross. He died before he was nailed to the cross. He wasn't nailed in that respect either, he was . . . his body was hung by ropes which were nailed. I see them driving spikes into the wood and then they tied the body to the spikes.

Bob: How did he die then?

Joe: Ah . . . I see intense torture—multiple beatings. I only identify with a strike to the head regarding that. I think he was struck in the head with an object.

Bob: Of what sense can you make of his death then?

Joe: Hold on a second and I'll try and find out.

(long pause)

Joe: Ah . . . have to create a place . . . or a . . . you have to create a parameter in which the higher experience can be experienced, in order to develop information based solely on the higher experience. Ah . . . it's kind of like . . . I'm trying to figure out a way of translating . . . of putting it . . . but I'm really having trouble doing this. Ah . . . it's like a . . . man until that point, or interaction between men created a form of learning or a form of information that was called learning, and this form of learning had become stagnated. It needed kind of a kick in the pants, in order to progress to the next level. So . . . the reason for his . . . his actions, were to . . . to initiate a question or a . . . a questioning that would grow as a blossom in the minds of men and women. It's sort of like promulgating a new . . . a totally new experience, or a new experiential type of thing that men would come to know, that would cause them to participate or interact on a higher level of what man was really supposed to be.

(long pause)

Joe: I'm trying to . . . I'm trying . . . be very . . . it's kind of like ah . . . man at the time was like two kids on the street corner. And their interaction at first is a discussion on who has the prettiest models or the best looking bike, or I bet I can jump out of that limb in the tree and you can't, etc. That . . . that form of interaction was producing a truth or information of certain level. So then, these two boys are met by a man, and the man says, have you ever wondered where that tree came from, or how it might have grown? And the boys find that in the next day they are discussing the more esoteric nature of the tree, or the possible manufacturer of the bicycle, or how marbles are made—it kind of like shoved them up to the next level of understanding, of curiosity. The interaction between them produces a truth that's a tenfold higher step than who has the largest bag of marbles—that kind of an effect. (long pause)

Joe: I feel a need . . . I just want to say one thing here. In the course or history of humanity this manifestation, this Being called Christ . . . well . . . that was one way of doing this . . . doing it. There are many ways of doing this . . . doing it. World War for example is another way of doing it. (long pause)

Bob: Can you explain that in more detail? Give us an example. What has this to do with this man Christ or Jesus who you are talking about?

Joe: OK. That may be a tough one. Hold on and I'll try and find out.

(long pause)

Joe: ex . . . even . . . (laughing) got a humorous answer here. Really fascinating as well . . . ah . . . first off, I have to say to you in exactly these words; that you Robert . . . that Robert Monroe already knows this answer. I don't know why, but I'm just supposed to tell you that. I'm also supposed to tell you that it was his best or own idea. Now this is something I don't understand myself. I don't know who or what is meant by this . . . or his. That's the message I got, and it was followed by a laugh (which caused me to laugh). Like a humorous thought, stuck into the middle of all of this. OK.

Bob: I'm not sure about that message. Can you tell me more? What about continuing on with this man Jesus you were speaking of earlier?

Joe: The only other thing that I can say is . . . I also get a flood of faces when I got that answer. Faces . . . none specifically . . . just . . . and not specifically human faces, more a presentation of identity, I guess—a multitude of identities. You know . . . not faces of faces, but . . . essences of identities I guess. I don't know what any of this means. I don't know why I'm getting this specific information now. What do you want me to do?

Bob: Tell us about the other ways—why not go back to the singular energy (beam) and tell us more about it.

(long pause)

Joe: OK. Suddenly I feel as though I'm being whipped around here quite a bit. You know . . . shaken somewhat . . . and . . . I'm trying to find out . . . but . . . ah

(long pause)

Bob: Find the energy (beam) and reach out and touch it . . . make contact directly if you can.

(pause)

Joe: I've got kind of a . . . ah . . . I've got a problem here.

Bob always joked about how I sounded like one of the astronauts that suddenly discovered there is a major leak in the capsule. Sort of a very downplayed "Gee Houston, I think I've got a problem here."

I've done that . . . I say the answer is yes, I can touch . . . it. But I'm suddenly in a different kind of operational mode here. It's a new . . . like a totally new . . . it's a new . . . ah . . . new . . . window? Yes, that's it . . . a new window or something. Very interesting . . . very interesting. It's like a totally different kind of window. It's suddenly evolved.

(long pause)

Joe: I don't feel like I have any control with this window. That's new . . . it's also very interesting. When I enter it (window), I feel as though I'm being blasted apart in all different directions. There's a way of doing this, but I'm not sure exactly yet how it's going to be. I'm trying to explain what I'm experiencing here. It's kind of like all these thought balls as you would call them, especially the ones in the past, are all linear, and then all of a sudden I'm dealing with thought balls that are horizontal as well as linear. There seems to be a spatial difference in these thought balls.

(long pause)

Joe: I just keyed into something else now that's really interesting. The coming together of two realities, isn't too far off in the . . . ah . . . the far-flung future. It's not too far off and that is apparently one of the reasons why the . . . this cogent Being has been going and coming over the years. There are two time tracks intersecting soon. (Soon in this case is relative to man's history, could be a year, could be a thousand years.)

Bob: Can you touch the energy in any way?

Joe: I don't know. I'll attempt to actually do that and see what happens . . . see what happens to the parameters here . . . the . . . I won't lie to you. I've never tried this before . . . so I'm having some degree of ambivalence, but that may be just crap I have to get out of the way.

(long pause)

Joe: That's it. OK. Hold on.

(very long pause)

Bob: Are you OK?

There was no response. Just a very long continued silence that Bob patiently waited through. He later told me that he was very concerned for me, as my breathing seemed to vanish and the biofeedback signals dropped to an unusually low reading. He toyed with the idea of going to the cube and shaking me back to reality, but decided that might generate a worse string of events.

Joe: OK. I'm back. It would appear that our historical record doesn't do justice to the man's intelligence. Ah . . . everything that is written in the book we call the Bible . . . the books within the Bible . . . are very shallow. Very shallow. There is an even deeper understanding that can be gotten from the book called Bible if you can just see past the garbage. In its entirety . . . it's a carrier of a larger message. In that respect it has survived . . . historically it has survived. There's a much larger message there.

Bob: Is there anything else I should know?

(long pause)

Joe: OK. That's it. I've got to turn on the light. That should do it I think.

(end of transcript)

As you can see, the explorer sessions were quite interesting and sort of open-ended. They are not the same as remote viewing, because Robert Monroe usually knew what the subject or topic was that he was seeking information on. This automatically voids the remote viewing protocol, even though he generally tried not to lead us in any specific direction.

He preferred "intent," getting a remote viewer to the target, and so allowed us to sometimes ramble in an explorer session, knowing that eventually we would get to where he wanted us to go anyway.

In the case of the Jesus transcript, I knew very early on that my perceptions were centered around the historical and religious figure of Jesus Christ. So, there is probably a lot of personal overlay mixed in with what I was trying to decipher from the experience. An interesting side note to this explorer session is that I had then, and have now, no recollection of anything that I said during the session. My only consistent memories of the events that transpired were the constant and overwhelming sensations of humor and joy. It was as if I were constantly in the presence of a truly happy and joyful being.

Origins

On November 29, 1983, I did another explorer session with Robert Monroe that dealt with the past, only it goes back about as far into humankind's history as I've probably been. I've included it to demonstrate just how far back in time one might go, and the interesting information that might be uncovered as a result.

The targeting material was contained within a double-wrapped, opaque envelope, with the following question written on a paper inside:

"From where did man originate? Describe the beginnings of man."

I was asked to go to my remote-viewing window—"The Library." Once there, I was asked to tell the monitor when I was ready. The monitor was Robert A. Monroe, and there were no other personnel within the lab during the session. The session lasted 129 minutes, including pauses, some that exceeded five minutes in length.

Joe: OK. I'm back in the Library.

Bob: Do you feel comfortable?

Joe: Very.

Bob: That's good. Reach out in the Library and find a book that will tell me what I want to know.

Joe: It's a dusty book and there seems to be a title on it. It says, "Earth." It's really fascinating. I'm now seeing a . . . ah . . . a collage of faces. And ah . . . I'm going back . . . I feel like I'm going back through history for something. And now I'm falling backward through this long tunnel that's filled with a collage of faces. Each representing a . . . ah . . . nationality or a period within time. I just keep . . . just falling through this tunnel and it's really fascinating. Almost like I could just stop and pick a specific period, time, or face and study it.

Bob: If you wish you can stop at any point that will answer the questions in the envelope.

Joe: Something just caught my eye. I guess I'll just remember where that is and come back to that later. I'll kind of fall then drift to your area of interest, whatever that might be.

Bob: Very good.

(long pause)

Joe: Get a interesting picture now. I'm on a . . . shoreline. Breakers and surf with lots of rocks sticking out of the water. They are very ragged rocks . . . like they're . . . they're like new in some way . . . edges still sharp—maybe volcanic. And there's ah . . . some . . . some kind of tribal clan . . . er . . . no. I've got to correct that. It's not a tribal clan at all. Ah . . . it's a family of sorts. A very large family . . . of . . . what appears to be some kind of animals . . . yes, I'd have to call these animals. I think anyway.

(long pause)

Joe: They are not at all like us, that is man . . . especially the way we look today . . . but there is a sense of man about them for some reason I can't be sure about. They are not like monkeys either. I would say ah . . . they are small. Not too tall, four feet maybe, very long hair, covering most of their bodies but it's like a . . . ah . . . it's like it's different . . . a different kind of hair. It's short, short in some respect in some areas, but long in others. Like the . . . long hair is decorative, or sex oriented, and the short hair is protective in some way.

(long pause)

Joe: These little guys are much like a . . . ah . . . sea otters. They're . . . are . . . ah . . . very native to the water . . . appear to be. Appear to be living mostly in the water. And they are coming up on the rocks to sun themselves. Eating in the rocks. Lots of grooming going on. I'm trying to pick out some features and I see a . . . I see foreheads and noses and parts of faces that are very humanlike to a certain extent. Not apelike or gorillalike at all. Just . . . ah . . . just a little different from modern man's characters. Cranial capacity of course looks to be quite a bit smaller. I wonder why they keep reminding me of man? Interesting. Can't seem to figure this out.

(long pause)

Joe: Sorry. Just a minute, I want to check something out here.

(very long pause)

Joe: Looking for a form of communication, and I . . . ah . . . and I'm not getting much of one except . . . there's an awful lot of touching . . . and . . . it seems the posturing of the head is extremely important. The way they hold their chin and there is . . . ah . . . a lot . . . of expression in the eyes. There is a lot of intelligence

in the eyes as well . . . again the man thing. They stand up-
right and I haven't seen any of them moving on all fours,
except for climbing. There seems to be quite a bit of simi-
larity to the movements, climbing and walking . . . almost
. . . almost as if they . . . these actions are strongly related in some way.

(long pause)

Joe: Another interesting thing is they . . . ah . . .
have a more extended webbing between the toes of the
feet . . . toes which are a little bit longer than they are
in us. The hands also have a definite webbing between
the fingers. Very efficient swimmers. Their nails are
very hard as well. Thicker . . . thicker nails, but a lot . . .
a lot longer. They have almost no hair at all on their . . .
ah . . . forehead and around the . . . ah . . . eyes and
nose. And ah . . . apparently the hair grows very short
on the facial area. I don't see any with long hair on the
facial area.

Bob: Can you communicate with them?

(long pause)

Joe: Just a minute . . . trying . . . trying to.

(long pause)

Joe: They alert like . . . ah . . . they . . . sense ah . . . the
direction the message is coming from. But, they don't see
me of course, they do . . . acknowledge . . . yes . . . that's
the word . . . They acknowledge me or at least a higher
communication. They are sort of . . . sort of half bending
over and just scanning or staring in my direction. They
don't seem to be abnormally excited, though. It's like they
can sense in multidimensional space or something—like
they are mystically-oriented creatures.

Bob: Nice. The implication is what?

Joe: I don't know. Let me find out what's next on the
agenda here.

(long pause)

Joe: Another interesting thing here . . . is that they ah . . .
they're afraid of the ah . . . they're afraid of the inside of
the jungle area or the ah . . . trees . . . the trees alongside

the beach. They are sticking to the edge of the shore . . .
not actually living in the water . . . but they're . . . right on
the water's edge . . . just like it's a form of security . . . or
they're . . . it's a comfort zone for them, probably an escape route. It's like they are playing off the land and sea,
one against the other for survival.

Bob: Good.

Joe: Let me see if I can find out anything else here that
I am supposed to be picking up on.

(long pause)

Joe: It's really interesting. I don't get much of anything
else going on here for some reason. I get ah . . . I get a . . .

(long pause)

Joe: I get an interesting . . . interesting presentation here.
There's a significance between the . . . there is a significance
in that the Earth is very, very primitive for some reason. And
there is a huge contest going on for control between species
on the land and control between those in the water. These
. . . this particular species of animal is put . . . specifically
in that barrier area . . . called the meeting of the land and
the sea. It's like they know they can participate in both
and are using it for survival and knowledgability. I also get
an impression that they're . . . ah . . . they were put there.
They mysteriously appeared. They are not descended
from a earlier species, they were put there.

Bob: Begs the next question doesn't it?

Joe: (laughing) I'm already asking that now . . . but am
not sure I'm getting an answer that I like.

(long pause)

Bob: Just report what you are perceiving.

Joe: Yeah . . . I'm getting an answer that ah . . . a seed
ship . . . no that's not right. Keep wanting to say a ship,
but it's not a ship. I keep seeing a . . . self . . . myself I
keep seeing . . . oh hell, for lack of a better word . . . let's
call it . . . a laboratory, where they are actually inventing
these creatures. They are actually constructing animals
from genes. Why would they be doing that? Can we do
this yet . . . here and now? Like cutting up genes and then

pasting them back together. You know, sort of like splicing plants . . . or grafting them, one to another.

(long pause)

Joe: Interesting. It's like they are building eggs by injecting stuff into them with a mixture of DNA or gene parts or pieces.

Bob: Who's the "they"?

Joe: I'm asking that too and I keep getting . . . hold on a minute. I keep getting nothing . . . but . . . ah . . . that may be my problem. Hold on a second and let me work on this a minute.

Bob: Very good.

(long pause)

Joe: I'm getting a . . . I'm getting a false picture here and I think it's a . . . it's an implanted picture. I'm getting an impression of a very aquiline-featured entity of extreme delicacy. Very much like a human being, except that there is a prehensiled tail, no evidence of clothing or sexuality. Doelike eyes . . . extreme . . . ah . . . fine boned, very long fingers . . . extremely long fingers, almost spiderlike. Hmmmm . . . I keep saying in the back of my head . . . is this they . . . "they"? And . . . I keep getting a no . . . it is more like an "I" or a "me."

Bob: Interesting. Then probe the I or me.

(long pause)

Joe: All I get is . . . ah . . . ah . . . all I get is like looking into a . . . like peering into a black . . . ah . . . oh . . . what I would translate as a . . . ah . . . perfect blackness. With an extremely bright flashing light . . . like a flashing light. The two are so absolutely perfect though, the white and the black. Flashing white is ah . . . very rhythmic and it has like . . . an aura coming out from a central point. Much like a new sun with a specific frequency or pulse.

Bob: Can you match that particular flashing . . . is it slow or is it fast?

Joe: Let me look. Let me count.

Bob: I can match it with a Hemi-Sync pulse if you wish and we can see how close we can get to it.

Joe: OK. Give me the pulse.

Bob began generating a Hemi-Sync pulse at this point and altering its speed or rate in an attempt to match the pulse that I was perceiving visually from a star field.

(long pause)

Joe: Hold it a second.

(long pause)

Joe: Slow it down just a little bit.

(long pause)

Joe: Hold it right there . . . right there.

(long pause)

Joe: Ah . . . that's it.

Bob: Very good.

Joe: It's really hard fighting it off when I'm hearing it, too . . . did you shut it off? Yeah.

Bob: No, not yet. What is the effect if you don't fight it off?

Joe: Let's find out.

Bob: OK. But, take it easy.

(very long pause)

Joe: Feel like my whole body has turned into pure energy. Heart rate has doubled. Makes me feel very excited. Feel like with each flash I'm expanding in some kind of way. As the flash goes away, I'm contracting. Evidently there is a direct line of some kind to an energy source which has a stamplike effect on life . . . ah . . . living beings. It's like a nuclear-driven lamp which has a specific energy signature or frequency signal that directly affects life. I know that's kind of hard to understand the way I've expressed it, but it's kind of a hard concept. It's like our Sun impressing us with a set frequency or broadcast of light for developmental purposes.

Bob: Do you feel comfortable enough to stay with it for a little while?

Joe: Yes.

Bob: Move closer if you can.

(long pause)

Joe: Oh for crying out loud . . . I can't believe it. Hah. I get a single cross corollary with this, Bob. It's a grow lamp, for Christ's sake.

Bob: It's a who?

Joe: (laughing) It's a grow lamp.

Bob: Describe what you are sensing more carefully.

Joe: It's a fucking grow lamp. There is a need for a stable energy source for some reason in this procedure . . . ah . . . in this lab . . . and this is like a generator for a stable energy. A simulation of sunlight, but on a grand scale of things. They are replicating the exposure from what one might call an M-Class planet's sun.

Bob: What's its source?

Joe: Like stepping into . . . in . . . to . . .

(long pause)

Joe: Like stepping into a huge undulating cloud or mist of . . . specks of color. I don't get anything from the cloud at all except for very vibrant colors.

(long pause)

Joe: There's an intelligence here, too . . . but I can't seem to get close to it or touch on it . . . I keep getting overwhelmed with confusion. There's got to be a different way of . . . ah . . . trying to . . . to . . .

Bob: Ask for help.

(long pause)

Joe: Get two messages . . . ah . . . keep getting shown the flashing light. And there is a message that comes with the . . . flashing light that says ah . . . nothing ever comes here. Yes. Interesting message. Nothing ever comes here. This is evidently a . . . some . . . an entity of some kind that's ah . . . like in charge of the lab . . . the ah . . . generating power? That actually sounds very simplistic . . . but that's what I keep getting. An entity . . . cloudlike in form that generates power. This cloud just is for that purpose . . . its whole goal in life. Life . . . like a sun has life. He, she, or it, isn't old or new. It's kind of like a . . . spark . . . explosion or beginning of some kind. An ectoplasm that just generates energy. I get the sense that it's sort of an explanation for how things begin.

Bob: What directs that energy?

Joe: Ah . . . wow. Hmmmmm. Ah . . . keep getting a very intense . . . a very intense charging when I do that. Like ah . . . pulling wires apart or something. Only these are hot wires. Now I'm back on the beach with the natives. Kind of interesting. I felt like I was being pulled apart. Like a very large . . . ah . . . very intense charging was taking place when I tried to penetrate that. And ah . . . all my wires were being pulled apart or something . . . similar . . . something similar to going back to a . . . a raw beginning.

Bob: What was the answer that you said you were getting that you didn't like? Do you remember now?

Joe: Ah . . . Yeah. There's a . . . I don't so much mind . . . but others might find it cruel. It's like someone tending a garden and planting the seeds. But apparently ah . . . I'm expecting a reason for that, a response that I'm getting however is that there really isn't any concern about the seeds after they are planted. Which is really kind of strange or even cruel. I don't detect a purpose. It's simply like . . . well . . . put these seeds here and on to better and bigger business. No concern about backtracking and checking on the condition of the seeds. They can live or die, survive or perish.

Bob: What period are we talking about here? What year would you say it is?

Joe: I'll see if there is something that I can associate this with here. So far there doesn't seem to be much of anything that looks even remotely familiar.

(long pause)

Joe: It's ah . . . the beach creatures are a much larger animal in comparison to most of the others. There's no large land animals in the area that I can determine over perhaps the size of a dog. Lots of very heavily armored land animals, by that I mean they are carrying shells, or have hard, crustaceous types of skin. There are some very large sea animals. But, no grass eaters yet. Plants appear to be large fungi instead of trees. I'd say it's . . . ah . . . at minimum . . . it's ah . . . ah . . . gosh I don't know . . . ah . . . at least thirty to fifty million years post dinosaur age. But I don't have any idea what that means in time. There's nothing that even remotely looks like a dinosaur on this planet, that is Earth.

Bob: Move forward in time then and tell me when you can clearly communicate with this creature.

(long pause)

Joe: A significant point occurs . . . ah . . . at two points. Two points occur that seem to cause a significant change in communication ability. Ah . . . first is, the shoreline is invaded by large animals. Major change in communications is what are apparently loud whistles. Almost like a *clucking* or *clicking* kind of a noise, like a coughing noise of some kind. It's been developed for signaling the presence of threat . . . warnings about larger animals . . . the presence of larger animals. Warnings. Giving locations through sound. Seems to be some sketching in the dirt as well. Like they are drawing things pictographically to represent things. Not letters or words but layouts of . . . layouts of position . . . characterization. Physical characteristics have changed significantly as well. These are now much heavier animals. More like man to a certain extent? A tremendous amount of muscular growth. Can this be man? Some kind of ugly if it is. That is ugly bodies, but nice faces. The ah . . . features are not as loosely drawn as in the smaller creatures . . . chest development has increased from moving and constructing things . . . maybe shelter? I don't know. Calluses down the feet . . . the webbing is beginning to lose ground. Upper shoulders and neck area is losing much of the hair covering. Many parts of the longer mane of hair is now gone. Backs of hands and arms losing hair. Second point of communications . . . significant change in communications is ah . . . they've gone from sea creatures and a sea source for food to hunting for small rodentlike animals on land using mostly traps . . . dead fall types of traps. Digging holes. First appearance in decorations as well, tying bits of fur to their body hair.

Bob: Go further forward in time.

(long pause)

Joe: OK . . . there seems to have been a profound change here . . . a very profound . . . ah . . . change. See a change occurring about the time of the loss of . . . perhaps about another million years. See tribalization. Gathering together of these creatures into groups, not just based on family structure anymore. Looking for a cause for that and I get a change in the . . . frequency of the flashing light. It's been increased. It's been speeded up. Light is also no longer intently white anymore . . . it's starting to get a slight tinge of yellow in it. Maybe the Sun is changing.

Bob: Let me change the Hemi-Sync speed and tell me when I've matched it.

Joe: OK.

(pause)

Joe: Right there! Back it up just a hair. That's good. Back it off just a little bit more. Hold it. Nope still not fast enough. Speed it up just a bit. Hold it . . . hold it. That's about right. Starting to lose it here. In watching this particular pulse rate, I just kind of started drifting here. Seems to be causing a bit of a problem with concentration and sort of . . . ah . . . wandering off. Might be seeing the ah . . . birth time of the duality of . . . what is this? The brain. Birth of the duality of the brain. What an interesting input. Wonder where that came from? Mind-brain aside. At least its (brain's) ability to function one side or the other . . . no that's not right . . . inside or outside. Prior to this point there was either no left/right brain communication, or no higher thing called mind. Two totally different functions were being performed within the same animal but with no correlation. A beginning of dual functioning and perhaps higher consciousness. Sort of like the birth of curiosity . . . yes that's the word.

Bob: OK. Move forward in time again.

Joe: OK.

Bob said I sounded like I actually went to sleep here for about fifteen minutes, then suddenly and inexplicably woke up.

Joe: Must have gone off somewhere, Bob. Can't remember what you asked me to do.

Bob: Move to a primary change.
Joe: OK.
(long pause)
Joe: Ah . . . very primitive Indians of some kind. Herd-following Indians, it would appear. Migrating. Migrate to live. Just see primitive Indians making temporary shelters . . . travel behind herds of game. Maybe some kind of gathering going on as well, hard to tell.

At this point, I drifted off to sleep in earnest. Bob turned off the equipment and left the lab. I woke up a couple of hours later, very well rested.

While the past may be very, very interesting to some, it is still science fiction to others. There are some very provocative statements contained within these two examples, which were done in 1983.

Talking about gene splicing or the alteration of DNA in 1983 is somewhat fascinating. And suggesting that changes in the Sun's frequency or pulse rate may be having a direct effect on the development of life, does give one reason to pause. However, a lot of the information departs quite radically from the norm, so as a result, could be quite threatening to some. Just the targeting of the past is a major departure from reality for most people. The in-your-face commentary of a remote viewing or explorer transcript usually runs counter to many people's beliefs. It certainly runs counter to what science and/or history might be saying at any specific point in time. All of which has a direct bearing on what most people might accept at any given time as reality.

Targeting the future opens even larger and more problematic doors to areas that one then has to deal with. To more clearly understand some of these difficulties, we first need to address some of the concepts surrounding future viewing.

[1] Signals designed to affect hemispheric-syncronization, thereby inducing an altered state condition.

7

CONCEPTS ABOUT FUTURE PREDICTIONS

When targeting the future, interesting things can happen to the material during collection. There are unique twists or sudden changes in direction that not only affect the remote viewing and data perception as it is taking place, but they are unique to future viewing and probably don't occur when targeting the past or present. The easiest way to illustrate some of these problems is to present them as examples.

Example One

Let's pretend for a moment that we are living in the year 1850, on the Great Plains of America. This is a place of rolling hills, grass, herds of cattle, and small, scruffy farms, where people are attempting to fight the grass to raise crops. In most cases, they're using the sod to create the homes they are living in.

Imagine now that we are part of a small team of men trying to herd cattle across this vast and open space. Some-where along the way, perhaps on his last trip to a town, one of the men who can actually read has picked up a tattered penny novel that contains an article on remote viewing. We decide that it would be a great idea to target such a remote viewer toward the future. Maybe we can get a leg up on everyone else by knowing what will happen before it actually happens. Maybe this remote viewer could even tell us a good place to dig for all that gold we've been hearing about out in California.

We're also lucky in a sense, because one of the men working with us—good ol' Frank, who has been riding drag all day and is the last man into camp that night—is currently recovering from a kick in the head by his horse. He almost died, but luckily is now recovering. Because he had a Near Death Experience, he's been having strange knowings since it happened, so we figure he'd make the perfect remote viewer.

So . . . we eventually make camp and we are all sitting around the campfire. We've had our dinner and the conversation has drifted into this thing called remote viewing. Good ol' George shifts over next to Frank and whips out a rough map of California. It's drawn rather crudely on a roll of deerskin. Since we know they've discovered gold in California, it is the perfect place to target Frank against. Maybe he can tell us where to find the big strike.

Following protocol, we don't tell Frank what we are specifically looking for. Instead, George jams his index finger down on the leather map and his nail hits a spot roughly somewhere in a place that doesn't yet exist, a place that will eventually be called Menlo Park.

"OK, Frank, tell us something really important about this spot in some future year. Something that has to do with big money."

Frank stares into the fire until his eyes roll back in his head. He makes a slight groaning sound. It is obvious he has entered a strange, somewhat altered, state. After a few seconds, he looks at us with eyes that seem to be peering off into a void, a never-never land of information. And he says, in terms or phrases none of us has ever heard before:

"I see partially vacated, yard-long tubes of glass five inches in diameter, connected to heavy iron-alloy turbinelike vacuum pumps. I hear high-pitched sounds of intense power outputs, and see fine wirelike cobalt-blue lights coming together in vials of gas, producing very small and narrow bolts of lightning, which are detonating down the glass tubes, striking something that looks like a thick rod of black diamond. The rays of light are shaving thin sections of diamond off like a hot knife through soft butter. The cuts are a hundred times thinner than a human hair."

We all sort of sit there for a second or two, in a kind of shock, before we leap to our feet and run over to check out Frank's saddlebags. We want to know what kind of cactus buds Frank's been mixing in with his beans. It is now quite obvious to us that Frank is certifiably nuts.

What kind of science fiction is this?

While it doesn't make any sense to us at the time, Frank has just given us a near-perfect description of a high-energy pump laser being used to cut silicone. Unfortunately, we haven't a clue what to do with the information.

One of the problems with remote viewing the future is that while you may sometimes get near-perfect remote viewing results, the information will usually make no sense whatsoever.

We will either disregard it completely because it hasn't met our preconceived notions or expectations, or it just won't fit in with any concepts we are currently familiar with.

Continuing to use a pump laser as an example, few know that there were probably six or seven newly industrialized nations prior to 1900 that actually possessed all the elements required to make and operate a laser. The elements they might have lacked they could have built. Had they successfully built one back then, it would have only been a few years' leap from demonstrating the light beam in a lab to cutting and welding steel in industry. There was only one reason why this didn't happen. It was because they were unable to *conceptualize* it.

What kind of an impact would there have been on industry if someone like Frank had existed around 1850? What kinds of changes would have happened that might have affected the industrial revolution? Could we have learned to cut steel or weld it with a beam of light?

Some say things are as they should be. Concept arrives when it is supposed to, usually in some mystical or magical way. But somehow, I feel that we should be looking just a shade deeper. When it comes to our future, it feels like it should be more important than that.

In the greater sense, it is my belief that we currently possess all that we will ever need to do anything we want. All we really need is to be open to the possibilities. Being open helps us to define the requirements, leads us in the discovery of the new kinds of materials we need, and assists us in processing how they might all go together. Being open allows for the possibility of *conceptualizing* our future.

So, there are major problems that can crop up when we decide to address the future, whether we are going out a hundred years to look at a not-yet-existing machine, or going out a thousand years to see what our future has in store for us. In either case, the remote viewing can be almost perfect, but actually understanding it will take a whole lot more in the way of effort—not an impossible task, but not an easy one either.

This is actually one of the reasons it has taken so long for this book to be written. Much of what I reveal about the future is not just based on information collected through remote viewing, but also required a great deal of insight. So in a psychic sense, I had to let the information sit and cook, sometimes for extended periods of time. Letting the information jell has helped to expose the sometimes hidden *concept* encapsulated within. By allowing the information to jell, I was able to more clearly understand it.

When you begin to deal with future predictions, the topic generates an unending supply of questions. Some may be more important than others, but they are all quite interesting.

People who doubt what you are doing are quick to respond with remarks such as the following:

> ➤ Predicting the future implies that the future is fixed. What about our free will? Doesn't that matter?

> ➤ So a possibility exists for multiple universes and parallel universes. How do our actions affect what's going to happen tomorrow? What about these multiple possibilities? How do you reconcile that?

> ➤ Bringing something concrete back from the future, like an idea or a concept that doesn't yet exist, must somehow violate our relationship with the future, or the future's relationship with the past. So, how can you do that? How can that happen?

> ➤ What about God? Certainly God has something to say about all this.

Most of these questions have been around since humans began thinking about the future and our relationship to it. They have certainly been the grist of many of the science fiction writers since the late 1800s. People throughout history have presented their theories and perceptions about time, both future and past, and how we may be interacting within it. Theologians have commented on their fixed or not-so-fixed perceptions of time and what it means when defining our relationship to God and the great mysteries surrounding our place or purpose for being here. Many religions bring karma into the picture; things like guilt, sin, and eventually our punishment or rewards are hinged on how we believe time operates, how lives are lived.

The thing to remember is that there are a lot of different ways in which to interpret what the future holds for us. The perceptions that I am now going to share are my own, based on what I have observed through remote viewing or in dealing with the paranormal. They are my views as they specifically relate to what I have experienced and my perceptions about time and/or our place within it. Since this is my understanding for how things might work, I must once again caution the reader that my views are always subject to change or modification from time to time. Nothing is forever.

The Fixed Future and Free Will

When a psychic or remote viewer predicts the future, many feel they are simply making a statement about how they think the future will be at a certain place or point within time. Because we do this doesn't guarantee we are going to be correct. In other words, predicting the future does not in any way guarantee its outcome.

Most would like to think that if I predict that something will occur at a specific location in the year 2023, I am giving my best guess about what I believe will be observed at that time and place. That doesn't automatically create a require-ment for it actually having to happen. I am only attempting to state something ahead of time and have it be more right than wrong. If what I say happens, then I have only suc-ceeded in correctly describing what I saw or perceived.

Some would argue that since I might have predicted it, I also participated in helping to make it happen—a nice hy-pothesis and one that may even be true. I discuss this crea-tive aspect of prediction in some detail in the next chapter. But, for now, let's look only at the prediction side of the coin and not the creation side. I think that may help to bring some clarity to the subject of predictions.

One has only to look at how many times a psychic or remote viewer is wrong to see that being psychic isn't a perfect system. There are a lot of predictions that have missed their mark. So, psychic functioning or remote viewing should not be made to appear to be more than what it actually is.

Aside from the creative aspects, the psychic or remote viewer will be right or wrong. If they are right, bully for them, and if they are wrong, then they are simply that, wrong—nothing more and nothing less. In other words, it's

OK to be right or wrong, and no one should castigate a psychic for being too much of either.

Dean Radin, Ph.D., in his book *The Conscious Universe: The Scientific Truth of Psychic Phenomena,* Harper, San Francisco, 1997, says it best when he compares the study of the paranormal to baseball or basketball. No one ever expects a baseball or basketball player to get it right one hundred percent of the time. A really good player is sometimes on and sometimes not. It's the season that matters.

OK, but what about free will?

Well, there may be a hidden seed or agenda within our natural human ability to make predictions. If by making a prediction we are in some way supporting or providing a basis for that future, helping in effect to create it, then I don't view this as negative or destructive to the exercising of free will. On the contrary. The act of predicting could then be considered, by definition, a flagrant display of free will in action.

My view of how this might actually be operating is outlined in more detail in the chapter titled "The Verne Effect."

Multiple/Parallel Universes

Multiple universes are probably a fact. We have only to look at and study human beings and cognition to see that multiple universes exist and are very real. Every man, woman, or child alive on the planet today lives within his or her own universe. It is a universe based on our observations and/or our experiences, which have been recorded by us from the moment of our conception. In this, no two human beings are alike.

Knowledge is personal, and is steeped within a personal understanding about what we have perceived. In some cases, the differences between us may be small and not very apparent, but in others there may be canyons of variance between what we each believe or think we know. All is constantly being mediated by our own personalized experience and personalized history files.

A good way to exemplify this would be to look at how we perceive the world around us. We are connected to what we perceive as reality through our six senses: taste, smell, touch, sight, hearing, and by our intuitive nature (our innate psychic sense).

Where one of these senses has been partially damaged or hampered, we will usually make up for it with a heightened ability in one or more of the remaining senses. These are the ways through which we interface with reality. It is our way of not only perceiving the universe around us, but it is our only way of understanding it.

So when we process something, we can honestly say we "know" something to be true, but it is only "we" that can know what our processing has presented us with. Congruent or like perception in others can only be assumed. If we make assumptions about what others have processed, we may be in error. We can share information and we usually do. But, the best that we can ever say about what someone else might understand about the world around them is that we "believe" what they are saying about it or their understanding of it. We can never know what they know anymore than they can know what we know to be true about this thing we call reality.

It is possible that many of us have actually come to know something that is the same, but this knowing will always be structured within the framework of our own more personalized universe.

So, yes, each of us is a walking universe. Self-contained, interacting perhaps, but always singularly different, one from the other.

This is part of what makes every human being so important to every other human being. Since our realities differ, sometimes radically from one to another, I can think of no better reason for sharing. It's the only way to stay balanced within time/space reality. It's also a good reason for spending more time "listening" than "talking."

If you are looking for other reasons to believe why this is so, you need look no further than the underlying causes of war, politics, science, or religion. We, the population of the planet, represent a legion of universes that have come together in loosely knit societies or groups of shared belief. It's how we define ourselves. In some cases, we are willing to live and die for these beliefs, so they must be quite important to this thing we call reality.

Multiple universes seem to support a predictive or paranormal ability. The case for parallel universes is a bit more difficult and is probably best addressed in a separate chapter.

Violating the Future

A number of years ago, I was asked to participate in an experiment proposed by Dr. Dean Radin, who was then located at the Consciousness Research Laboratory, University of Nevada, Las Vegas.

He proposed using remote viewing to go into the future to obtain information concerning a machine that was not yet existent. We weren't sure at the time as to how far into the future this might require traveling, but the machine he conceptualized certainly did not yet exist.

What is important to note here is that we were in fact partially successful in this attempt. Since it is still an ongoing experiment, it is impossible to tell what the eventual outcome for this entire process might be.

We have been able to bring back some small elements or parts of the machine that seemed to work, at least the way they were envisioned. Not surprisingly, they do not yet do what he has conceptualized, but instead have opened some rather unusual doors to other prospective areas. Some of these might yet produce a patentable idea. Unfortunately, I am unable to discuss this in any detail, as it is proprietary and still under development.

By doing this, have we somehow broken some existent rules or laws that somehow govern the future? No. It may be that Dean will eventually be successful in creating a completely new machine based, at least in part, on remote viewing. If so, then the existence of the machine within the future may simply be a direct result of what we are doing now.

It is not a violation of future ethics, it is simply a variance on the act of creativity. This is how creativity works. It is how all new things come into existence. I've just put a paranormal label on it.

New ideas are conceptualized, thought about, then attempts are made to bring them into reality. How far you are willing to peer into the future and your ability to act on the information, is the seat of power that exists within almost all of the current research, experimental engineering, and cutting-edge labs on the planet. What is surprising to me is that so many of them have not yet caught on to remote viewing.

I am not unique in this perception, or in trying to implement psychic or remote viewing ability in support of new or creative ideas. There are now labs that exist in many countries that are attempting to use remote viewing techniques to gain a foothold on the new technologies of tomorrow. What saddens me is that most of America still believes these remote viewing abilities to be frivolous, unscientific, or a waste of time.

The "giggle factor" associated with remote viewing or psychic functioning continues to block earnest attempts at using these abilities for humankind's benefit (at least within America). Will we have to wait until some other nation or group of people proves remote viewing has value before we will open to the possibility of using it?

I can't help but think that historically this is how we wound up behind the power curve in the early days of the space race, or why we will probably not be the ones who are going to discover the new machines that are going to replace the computer systems of today. What's going to provide clean and unlimited power to meet our needs in the world of tomorrow? It's already sitting out there waiting to be targeted. Wake up, science.

What was learned early on about remote viewing may be the very reason Hal Puthoff, Ph.D., a man who was instrumental in the beginning investigations of remote viewing at SRI-International, has since struck off on his own in an attempt to address some of these problems. He has produced some very interesting papers on energetic vacuums, the production of energy from nothing, and the velocity-of-light limitations to the Alcubierre warp drive. These issues may one day have an astounding impact on humankind. It may be too early to know, but my gut tells me that he is probably on to something, and certainly remote viewing helped.

This is an important issue. Corporations in America have the means and money to set up or endow research that could support a study of the experimental applications of remote viewing or psychic functioning to creativity, but at present it seems they lack the fortitude or long-range vision necessary to take the risk. Hopefully this will change in the near future.

As a research associate with the Cognitive Sciences Laboratory of Palo Alto, I can say that we stand on the threshold of discovery. We possess an astounding array of experience, capability, and ideas that directly affect this problem. Anyone seriously interested in doing something in this area should contact me, or Dr. Edwin C. May, the director of the lab.

What about God?

My experience with remote viewing and nineteen years of investigation into the paranormal have only underscored the near pristine beauty and veracity of God's involvement within what we call reality and its creation. I look on God as the Grandest of Engineers, the power behind the movement of stars in the one extreme, to warm winds on a summer night in the other. It is our spiritual relationship with God that brings purpose to our interface with reality.

Remote viewing, or psychic functioning, or any talent we humans possess, is a reflection of the Engineer. Such belief clearly supports the idea of free will and it underscores the direct role we play in carrying out the ultimate or grand design.

Because we play such an important role, it is dependent on us to use it within a framework of understanding that has as its base our theological beliefs. We live with the results of our actions. It therefore requires us to understand the ethical and spiritual responsibilities we carry as the Grand Engineer's creations here in physical reality. These are not responsibilities that should be taken lightly. Since we do exercise free will in all of the decisions and actions we carry out on a moment-to-moment basis, we are directly responsible for the changes or effects of these actions, or in some cases, inactions, on reality.

These can range from the simple, ignoring the plight of a single individual, to the more complex, learning to split atoms, and the creative or destructive power that might bring to generations of human beings.

Therefore, it should be a requirement that in understanding how our actions might have an impact on the world around us we not make any decision without at least reflecting on our spiritual responsibilities to our fellow human beings.

One of the great truths that I have learned over the years is that we will most definitely experience what we set into motion through our actions. All of our actions directly affect all that exists within our reality.

Constructive or positive expenditures of energy seem to produce a constructive or positive reality. Destructive or negative expenditures of energy seem to produce a like effect. It is, therefore, not only beneficial for us to try and understand our spiritual nature, to try and mediate what we do, to exercise some degree of control, it is imperative.

The theological ideals and hypotheses surrounding our spiritual and/or religious nature are essential if we are to be able to grasp our role within the universe at large. We are all the creations, the children, of the Grand Engineer, and the Grand Engineer has given us the means to both understand reality as well as to manipulate it within its proper context.

I have long since given up on the restricted sense of spirituality that comes from narrowed viewpoints regarding God, especially viewpoints that seem to underscore "requirements" associated with a particular church, sect, belief, or condition.

In my own mind, humankind expresses the need for spiritual awakening in all of the extant religions and religious practices that exist today. Judaism, Confucianism, Hinduism, Buddhism, Christianity, and Islam all speak to a belief in a higher order of understanding. Each essentially carries the same message—there is a Grand Engineer and we should know something about what that means. We should attempt to reach an understanding about what kind of responsibility that gives us as an integral part of creation.

Unfortunately, many still get sidetracked with the details. Wars are fought and weak excuses are made for atrocities based on these differences of details. An abomination, which only humankind suffers from. One of our worst creations. We are in charge of our reality, and we have only ourselves to blame for the actions that produce such waste.

I can't help but think the Grand Engineer didn't see this as a possibility. Maybe the fact that we create our own reality is the toughest lesson of all for us to learn and that is why it has taken so long to pull ourselves up to a point of seeing the possibilities.

We all live in a separate universe. Maybe it is time to see and understand that it is the confluence of these universes that constitutes the reality we will always experience.

8

THE VERNE EFFECT

To further underscore the impact of being able to conceptualize and to understand something about future viewing, one needs to look at those who have come before. None so readily exemplifies future viewing, or predictive paranormal functioning, as Jules Verne.

Jules Verne in 1863 began writing with intriguing detail about things to come. In great detail, he described the inventions of tomorrow. He projected cities, places, and things from his imagination, things that were not yet a reality in his time.

Within a single novel, *Twenty Thousand Leagues Under the Sea*, he foresaw the full development and impact of the submarine, the aqualung, fully automatic rifles, television, and space travel. He described recessed and indirect lighting, extensive use of fish farming, night vision devices, the electric clock and cooking, salt-water distillation using electric current, the idea of twin-hull designs, even the lock-out chamber now functional on nearly all production submarines.

Where did all this information come from? Certainly, his ideas far outstripped what was commonly known at the time that he was putting them on paper.

The actual concept of a submarine wasn't unknown. It had first been envisioned by an English mathematician named William Bourne in 1578. Cornelius Drebbel constructed a craft capable of submerging and resurfacing in 1620. And the first successful use of a submarine as a warship occurred in 1864, when the Confederate craft *Hunley* blew up the Federal corvette *Housatonic* in the Charleston Harbor on February 17, 1864. All of this occurred six years before his book was published. One might therefore argue that his future envisionments of the submarine were really good guesses, information extrapolated from what was already known. Or was it?

When you read his book, you quickly find that it isn't just the mention of a submarine that brings power to his predictive writing. He puts the submarine solidly within the context of a complex social structure and society, from which he then draws many other predictive objects, events, and conclusions. He thoroughly describes the details surrounding the times, which allows for a complete understanding of his concepts and ideas, as portrayed through his major characters.

Was he discerning objects and events not yet relevant to history—was he being clairvoyant? Or, was he stepping into the future with his mind and *seeing* that which was yet to come? Was he remote viewing?

Skeptics who are still arguing over the veracity or reality of remote viewing might call his predictions luck. This is not a surprise.

Lead-sealed targeting envelopes stored in private safes, a metanalysis of dozens of independent scientific studies, hundreds of evaluations, an entire army of scientists and oversight committees focused on providing protection against fraud, and periodic reviews for over a twenty-five-year period cannot seem to persuade those who will always find a reason to doubt the existence of the paranormal.

However, over the course of my experience within the classified remote viewing project, there are literally hundreds of examples of future targets (objects, events, or locations) that, in effect, didn't yet exist when the remote viewing material was created, assessed, and analyzed. In some cases, these targets could not even be verified as "coming into existence" for a period of nearly two decades. Why? Because they existed only in the future.

A few examples of such targets taken from the STAR-GATE files follow:

➤ The predicted launch date for a newly constructed submarine—110 days before it actually rolled from its construction crib and into the harbor.

➤ The predicted release of a hostage in the Middle East and a correct description of the medical problem precipitating his release. This information was provided three weeks prior to even the hostage takers knowing what they were going to do.

➤ A prediction of an attack on an American Warship: the location, the method, and reason for the attack—three days prior to the attack taking place.

When remote viewers look into the future, they can actually capture the energy, feelings, and *concepts*, and paint them on the canvas of our minds.

I've italicized concepts here, because this is probably the most important thing a remote viewer can perceive. As I've discussed previously, concepts are what integrate or tie the details of our visions together. They help us to understand what is going on in a different place in time, long before we ever get there. Concepts interconnect and weave the social and physical aspects of future sight into a framework or context that can be more easily understood by those of us trying to understand what a future prediction might mean.

Jules Verne was probably doing excellent remote viewing when he described the drive unit for his submarine in *Twenty Thousand Leagues Under the Sea*. All we have to do is emulate his work and look ahead ten, twenty, even seventy-five years, to pick and choose among the already existing miracles of technology. Sounds easy.

But is it?

I believe Jules Verne discovered very early on that understanding the conceptual framework was even more important than the details within his predictive perceptions. It is these very concepts that he brings to us in his writings that continue to amaze readers even today. He made the future so clear for us.

He also put the readers where they could imagine themselves to be. He never took us *into* the future, he brought the future back to us. He did this with a positive and creative impact, which we still feel today.

Jules Verne was born in Nantes, France, on February 8, 1828, and he died on March 24, 1905. Much to our benefit, in a period of less than a dozen years (1863-1874), he laid much of the foundation for what we know today as Modern Science Fiction.

Following his first acclaimed success (the novel *Five Weeks in a Balloon*), Verne presented a new manuscript to his publisher. The title of the manuscript was *Paris in the Twentieth Century* (1863). But Verne's publisher, Pierre-Jules Hetzel, was disappointed. In his own words: "I did not expect something perfect. But I expected better. My dear Verne, if you were a prophet, no one would *believe* your prophecies today."

The publisher warned that attempting to publish this new manuscript would be "a disaster" for both of them.

What were the prophecies that caused such a negative reaction? Why wouldn't the publisher produce his manuscript? Some of the details Verne provided in his new manuscript spoke about the year 1960. In it, he described travel by subway, gas-driven cars (the combustion engine was not built until 1889), communication by fax and telephone, the use of calculators and computers, and *electric* concerts providing entertainment. In his manuscript, he talked about a world in which everyone can read, but no one reads books! Latin and Greek are no longer taught in schools, and the French language has been filled with very "disagreeable" English words. Society is dominated by money, and the homeless walk the streets. It is a police state run by bureaucrats. He *imagined* streets overrun with lights and electronic advertisements. He even predicted the invention of the electric chair (which didn't appear until 1888).

Where did these ideas originate? Did he actually go into the future and *see* what was going on? Or, by envisioning such a future, did he have a hand in creating it? What if the imagination, the seat of creativity deep within the mind, is directly connected to what we might call "the eventuality of truth?" What if humankind is connected in a some psychic way with what is eventually going to happen?

In other words, what if we are capable of seeing or envisioning what we (humankind) will eventually *experience?* If this is so, then our perceptions of the future and all that it holds in store for us become an exciting, dynamic, and *interactive* adventure. We become *the ultimate time machine*, the ultimate traveler in time, by virtue of our ability to simply conceptualize it.

For a while, the scientists studying remote viewing hypothesized there might be a way that information could be passed to us—by us. One of the things they noticed was that *post hoc* feedback about the target and the results of the remote viewing seemed to have a dramatic effect on the percentage of time a remote viewer was right about a target, or the amount of information that could be collected or stated correctly.

A rather simplistic example of how this might happen is as follows.

On January 1, 1997, we envision an event. Let's say it is the discovery of a cure for AIDS. In our vision, we see a stark announcement in three-inch black letters embossed boldly across the headline of a newspaper—**CURE FOR AIDS DISCOVERED!** In our vision on the upper right-hand corner of the same newspaper, we see that the date is sometime in November of the year 2001. We write about it, and it is published as a "prediction." An incorrect term in all probability, but nevertheless, it is published.

A few years have now gone by, and we've forgotten about our vision. We are on the way to work and we stop by the newspaper kiosk and buy a copy of the local newspaper to read while on the train to work. Once comfortable in the train seat, we pull the paper from our briefcase and snap it open to the front page. There, embossed across the front page in bold black letters is the statement—**CURE FOR AIDS DISCOVERED!** Our reaction is to quickly glance at the upper right-hand corner of the paper, where we see the date, November 1, 2001.

The first assumption by most readers is that this is a correct "prediction." What the scientists hypothesize is that at the moment of cognition—where we suddenly understand a cure has been found—we actually *send the information to ourselves in the past!*

It is a full loop of cognitive communication. The entire communication, from when we first made the prediction until our complete feedback has all essentially taken place within ourselves. It is actually a complete event (except for the beginning—a remote viewing and the end—sitting on a train and reading the paper) that we experience outside of space and time, or within our minds.

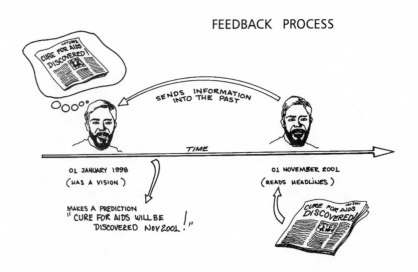

FEEDBACK PROCESS

SENDS INFORMATION INTO THE PAST

TIME

01 JANUARY 1998
(HAS A VISION)

01 NOVEMBER 2001
(READS HEADLINES)

MAKES A PREDICTION
" CURE FOR AIDS WILL BE
DISCOVERED NOV 2001 !"

CURE FOR AIDS DISCOVERED

While this view held sway for many years within the research community, at least with some of the scientists, I'm not so sure this is what was happening with Verne, nor with remote viewing. The counter argument is simple. Jules Verne died before he received feedback on most of what he predicted. So there must be something else going on here.

As a long-term and experienced remote viewer, it is my belief there are other possibilities to explain what is going on. These need to be examined.

Reality Constructs

What comes first, the chicken or the egg? The vision or the reality? My own perception is that reality is always a construct that first begins in the mind. It is a construct born from both my belief as well as my knowing. Philosophically, and as I've previously argued, one could state that we can never really *know* what someone else knows. We can only *believe* what they are telling us. Simply put, we are each stuck within our own universe of experience. Our realities have to be constructed from what we know to be true (usually a result of our own judgment, based on experience), and what we are willing to believe might be true (beliefs shared with us from others). If this is so, then each of us represents a separate universe or construct of reality. Because each of us probably represents a separate universal understanding of what reality is at any given moment in time, the world as we understand it either has to be a place of utter confusion, or it must be operating according to some additional rule, perhaps some form of consensus.

Fred Alan Wolf, in his book *Parallel Universes* (Simon and Schuster, 1988), somewhat touches on this when he says: "The fact that the future may play a role in the present is a new prediction of the mathematical laws of quantum physics. If interpreted literally, the mathematical formulas indicate not only how the future enters our present but also how our minds may be able to 'sense' the presence of parallel universes." He goes on to state, "The laboratory of parallel universe experimentation may not lie in a mechanical time machine, à la Jules Verne, but could exist between our ears."

To observe the truth in these statements, you only have to observe the people around you. You will see that some people are willing to believe in almost anything, while others believe in almost nothing they haven't touched, tasted, or personally observed. Some are viewed as reasonable in what they believe, but this is only because they fall within an acceptable line or boundary of agreement that's socially acceptable. Many are easily lured across this line into thinking they know something they don't, while others are quick to believe in anything, and are rather fixed with regard to what they actually know, or think they know. What is important here is the distinction that while we live in a multiple-reality universe, it is up to each of us to determine where we will draw the line between believing and knowing. So whether or not we like it, by its very construction—reality then becomes both a place of consensus as well as individuality. The degree to which we are allowed our individuality is dependent on the degree to which we are willing to accept personal responsibility for our own beliefs, thereby consciously affecting the consensus.

The kicker is that this consensus is probably an unconscious consensus and not a conscious one. That would seemingly agree with C. G. Jung's ideas surrounding the *collective unconscious*.

How This Might Work

In reality, at least as I envision it, most of what happens is based on an assumed order. For lack of a better word, I will call this assumed order the Unconscious Consensus. For the most part, we spend a great deal of time within our reality focused only on those things that directly affect us: finding a parking space for our car, shopping, studying, working, or being involved in the myriad relationships that are closest to us. These are certainly important issues for us in a personal sense, but within the larger view—or within the overall reality of our world or where it might be going—we are essentially turning over our personal responsibility toward creating the future to the "assumed order" or the Unconscious Consensus. So the world moves merrily along its path and we are subject to edicts by the Unconscious Consensus, which constitutes our overall reality construct.

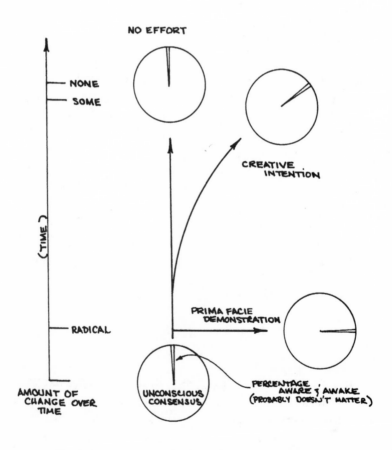

This implies that by virtue of the Unconscious Consensus, reality doesn't need us focusing on it in for it to exist. It operates automatically. It also implies that reality will quickly present objections to our beliefs whenever we happen to wake up or take notice in an awareness sense, and attempt to deliberately stray from within the boundaries of the Unconscious Consensus reality. So, reality, or the order in it, seems to exist very well without our help.

Let us further suppose that since reality seems to exist without any one of us at any given point in time, then past, present, or future, in all of their possible permutations, must also exist. In other words, reality just is!

Actually, this is already somewhat supported by how we actually enter or leave our world reality in the first place. When we are born, we sort of pop up within consciousness in what is seemingly an already existent reality, a holistic and viable universe. It initially doesn't hold much meaning for us, because we have to learn experientially what its parameters are. By observing events and interrelated objects, we eventually create a string or linear file of information. We call this string of observations "time." At first we don't understand time, but we do quickly learn to position ourselves within it. We create a historical record of what we have seen or experienced (know to be true), and a present record against which we can compare the historical record to maintain our rather tenuous grasp on the Unconscious Consensus. Since everything we know, versus believe, hinges on our experiential learning, it soon becomes a well-integrated history file, and supports our grasp on reality. Real-time observations or experiences, and our history file, always support our current point of reference in space/time. This creates an illusion that our place in reality is pretty much fixed within time, and is thereby in total agreement with the Unconscious Consensus view of reality. It also supports the unspoken belief that we will always be *subject* to the Unconscious Consensus, which may not actually be true.

So what about the future? Is it something we therefore only allow ourselves to contemplate, or on occasion do we allow ourselves to conceptualize it—make it happen? How does change occur?

I believe there are at least two ways that we can bring immediate change to reality, that is, alter the Unconscious Consensus. One method is rather dramatic and one isn't. Both reside within our perceptions about how the future operates, and how we understand our connection to it. In both cases, we can actually alter reality. We can change the Unconscious Consensus and mold it to the way we want it to be!

Bucking the System

The first and most dramatic way to affect an overall change in reality, or the Unconscious Consensus, is through an overt act that deliberately violates our historical file and current reference point regarding reality, or what the Unconscious Consensus is currently dictating as necessary.

In other words, an individual decides to make something happen that can be observed or participated in experientially by others, which in turn changes worldwide belief or knowing. A sort of in-your-face departure from what has commonly been accepted until that point in time. But it has to be a demonstration that cannot be refuted, such as the following:

On December 17, 1903, Orville and Wilbur Wright made history's first powered, sustained, and controlled airplane flight from level ground without assistance at takeoff. They were two of probably less than a couple of dozen serious inventors attempting to be the first to fly. At the time, most of humanity (the Unconscious Consensus) was stuck within the belief "If God meant man to fly, he would have created us with wings and given us feathers."

Where and when did the Wright Brothers' ideas or concepts for building an airplane begin? Some believe that Wilbur was influenced by Otto Lilienthal's successful gliding experiments in Germany in the 1890s, or perhaps by observing how buzzards maintained their balance while in the air. But while no one is absolutely sure, it could also have been by an idea—a vision for a new reality. Perhaps it was a small but tenacious idea or vision that was unconsciously planted within Wilbur's mind while a student in school. The idea, or vision, could have come from seeing pictures drawn by another man, also a visionary, who lived in the Republic of Florence from 1452 to 1519. His name: Leonardo da Vinci.

Regardless of the source or the earliest influence, what is important here is the fact that it didn't take approval from the Conscious or Unconscious Consensus to radically change an entire world view or pattern. It only took a "belief" concerning the future held by a few. Orville and Wilbur provided an "experiential observation," an in-your-face demonstration, which left little doubt in anyone's mind where belief left off and knowing began.

So, for a single instant in space/time, nearly all of humankind was suddenly and keenly aware of flight. It was at that point that the Unconscious Consensus made a sharp right turn, and was permanently and irrevocably changed. Suddenly, humans could fly.

Creating the Future

Through many years of incredible effort, Orville and Wilbur were able to affect a single belief. They made it a known. But there is also another way, another method, to directly affect the beliefs of many. There is a way to shake and mold the future before it actually happens, which may not be quite so dramatic, but which is certainly just as effective.

I believe Jules Verne understood this method, as do a handful of others within history. It is the ability to conceptualize, to envision a future *that already exists*—exists within the mind. The effect of future visions, whether by Jules Verne or another, will be twofold. Those who accept or believe in the visions will be opening a door. They are help-ing to conceptualize and create a future where things they have envisioned may one day come true.

On the other side of the coin are those who can't or won't open to new possibilities, who are essentially building walls across the road of progress. They are in effect restrict-ing man's evolution and birthright, strangling the fruit of the vine. The point to remember is that predictive ideas or con-cepts, while subtle, are enormously powerful.

To illustrate, how many engineers who volunteered to participate in putting a man on the moon read Jules Verne's *Journey to the Moon* in their youth? Did that prepare them, at least psychologically, for their challenge? Predictive ideas gather momentum like snowballs rolling down a mountain-side. Eventually they overwhelm and cover anything stand-ing in their way.

Predictions or Creations?

What about Verne's lost manuscript that has been recently found? Only Verne and his publisher read it. How could that have affected change within the Unconscious Consensus?

I believe we live in a world where reality exists as a condi-tion of the whole, where there is an illusion that the Uncon-scious Consensus rules and we feel we have no control over it, when in actuality we do. Some of us are awake and par-ticipant, while some of us choose to sleep. But we are all still inherently responsible for what is going to happen through both our actions as well as our inactions.

Reality is a fertile garden, ripe for new ideas. Thoughts by virtue of consciousness automatically become part of this whole—in fact, they are the very essence of what drives it.

It's really not that difficult to see where change comes from. I have simply to ask which came first, the handheld communication device on *Star Trek,* or a fluke idea that resulted in cellular phones?

One of our basic abilities to modify the future, our future, lies within our very own hands. It is the penultimate expression of free will. It is our ability to conceptualize, not just conceptualize as in a fantasy, but to place the future of man within a context of believability not yet material or realized.

Where a single human being can conceptualize a cure for cancer, there will be thousands who can capture the vision and believe in its outcome. Visionary writers like Jules Verne and current-day psychics who are able to share their visions in a proactive sense, create rallying points within the Unconscious Consensus. They are sparks of light that awaken people to the possibilities. They perform an important service to mankind, by looking beyond the walls of our current place in reality. They stretch their vision beyond the safety of current belief and dare to envision a reality that lies out there, somewhere, waiting for us. Through their writings and predictions, they help create and develop the very context or soup within which strange and new ideas can take seed. These strange and new ideas are the seeds of our future. It is out of this future that humankind's hope is born. It is the power and vision to change the world, to make it a better place in which to live.

I believe we are responsible for this future. But I also believe we fear it. We fear it because many believe we are "subject" to it, instead of having some control over it. Have heart. All the evidence points to the latter. Our future—in fact, this very book—is birthed out of what we are willing to believe is possible. Our future is thoroughly within our grasp. We need no longer be subject to it, we have only to envision it to break out of our reality cage.

By our thoughts alone, we are capable of generating reality and controlling what is going to happen to us. We have only to clean up our act and begin to envision the positive changes possible instead of focusing on the negative. I predict that Jules Verne had a clear understanding of this process, and so will others.

Given such a responsibility, we are almost required to look at the future with promise, with a positive attitude, not with the apprehension and dark vision that most would associate with the unknown. The future and what it will contain is truly within our hands. We should address it in light of the fullest expression of our power.

9

LOOKING INTO THE FUTURE

Because I view predicting the future as being an intentional act of creation, I approach it with a deep sense of responsibility to my fellow human beings. Stepping outside the Unconscious Consensus and attempting to influence what might be waiting down the road requires some degree of caution. There are a number of very good reasons for this.

First, while I would like to feel that I have had a direct part, albeit a small one, in creating the future, my conscious and corporal existence may be long extinguished from the physical by the time many of the predictions have come to pass. So I want to be careful about what I may have helped to create for others.

Also, I view the process of writing this book and its predictions as a deliberate and meaningful test of the efficacy of psychic functioning, remote viewing, and its part in the creation of a specific future. If a large portion of what I say happens, then perhaps it will influence or foster a greater belief in the role remote viewing can play in the development of our reality—a critically important message, in my opinion.

Lastly, this is a modest attempt to keep at least one copy of my book in existence until the end of the predictions, the year 3000. I would be less than honest if I were to deny the natural desire to extend my influence beyond a physical lifetime. Like most artists, musicians, and especially writers, I want to see my work survive.

During the past few years, there have been a lot of psychics, seers, scryers, and even remote viewers who have spoken about the future. They have usually restricted themselves to a few dozen years, the next century, or centered their predictions around the beginning of the next millennium. Almost exclusively, their predictions and perceptions focus on the "negative" or "crisis" types of events.

There are predictions for earthquakes, floods, major land shifts, sudden rises in water levels, runaway population growth, explosive wars, the spread of pestilence, new diseases, and even pathogens coming from space. All manner of dire and dangerous epochs of doom are being predicted as unavoidable.

Sadly, quite a bit of what has been predicted is probably going to be true. It is a fact that we live on a planet that spins through space, circling a medium-sized sun, within a whole galaxy of other systems, each with its own set of planets, all of which is quite vulnerable to circumstance. We need to understand that, within the vagaries of possibility, we have always been at risk, and that sometimes the risk is high.

I believe that my home, planet Earth, is a living, breathing entity—many don't—and that we are like parasites trying to ride and live on what is virtually a cosmic speck of matter zooming through space. The fact that we exist and can extend our consciousness beyond our immediate surroundings is a miracle of creation in itself. We are one of the Grand Engineer's marvels, probably one of many.

Earth is and always has been subject to certain cycles and changes that evolve from the fact that it is a living and breathing entity. While the Native American Indians and many other cultures acknowledge this, modern civilizations have for some reason chosen to look upon the globe as a place to control, to cut up, divide, and pump clean of its resources.

We think of it as a place where we can be in charge of ourselves. In our attempt to control, we have created institutions to address problems of weather, water, geology, ecology, and other Earth patterns in the hope that we can predict, alter, or change the course of these effects upon our existence. This has simply created an illusion of control. The truth is, we control nothing.

So, it is relatively easy to predict that there will be more earthquakes in the 8.0 range or higher. There will continue to be megalithic volcano eruptions that exact huge costs in property damage or the loss of human life. As we continue to populate and spread humanity across the globe, we are beginning to live where we probably shouldn't. Humanity continues to waste what we have always assumed is replenishable, and to quickly forget the lessons of the past.

As long as we insist on doing whatever we want, instead of what we should, we will continue to suffer the consequences. Hurricanes, tornadoes, floods, drought, and other climatic Earth cycles will continue to ravish us. They certainly aren't going to go away, and believe it or not, we are not going to control them at any time in the near future.

While this paints a pretty dark picture, there is a solution, although it may seem impossible. Like it or not, we have to come to some agreement about our vulnerability then make the necessary changes in our society to stop stealing from our future. It is no longer a matter of "if" we should be paying attention to these things. It is a matter of "we now have no choice," if our species is going to survive.

Because I view most of these natural events as a growing part of the norm, I certainly can't ignore them. But I will focus on them in the predictions only when I see them as being very significant to the evolution of our species.

Using earthquakes as an example, on any given day in the world there are probably over 300 earthquakes—some felt, some not. It is only reasonable to assume that as population centers continue to expand, and humanity shifts across the globe, more individuals will be experiencing these ground-shaking events and the damage that accompanies them. In some cases, you can point to specific areas of the world where, sometime in the next hundred years, tens of thousands will die, as a direct result of a significant earthquake.

They are easy to predict. Japan, parts of eastern Russia, the West Coast of the United States, and the eastern shores of the Mediterranean are just a few. These are earthquake centers because the plates and magma of the Earth are shifting and those plates are constantly moving. There is nothing mankind can do about it. The possibility of such an occurrence in any one person's lifetime remains approximately the same. This holds true whether you were born seventy years ago, were born yesterday, or thirty years from now.

People living at the base of large and active volcanos are also at high risk. Predicting another Krakatoa is relatively easy. Yes . . . there probably will be another eruption the size of Krakatoa or Mount Vesuvius, and it will occur within the next hundred years. It will most certainly take place within the "Ring of Fire" as the Pacific Rim area has been so aptly named. It might occur in the northwestern United States, the Aleutian Island chain, or off the coast of Borneo. People who live near or at the base of large and active volcanos in these areas are simply betting a pleasant view or peaceful lifestyle against suddenly finding themselves in the line of fire. Again, it is not a question of *if* one of these will occur; it is a question of *when*.

10

FORWARD TARGETING

In my attempts to collect sufficient data about the future and develop accurate predictions, I've actually compiled the material from many different sources.

The primary source, of course, is remote viewing. Most of the data about the near future, the present through the year 2100, comes from the files of remote viewings I've done over the past ten years; comments I've made based on these remote viewings at various seminars, talks, and presentations; as well as *post hoc* analysis of my own results. That is, where I've noticed obvious connective tissue that seems to string information from one remote viewing to another. Some of the viewing has also been recent and specifically tasked to answer some of the questions most often asked about the future.

Sometimes the circumstances surrounding the production of the information are not ideal, in that I am doing my own analysis or creating my own targets, but when addressing the future in a predictive way one is left with few alternatives.

In such cases where I've had to devise a method for targeting to preclude front-loading (previous knowledge about the specific target), I've written the dates with a targeting phrase on three-by-five cards and sealed them within opaque envelopes that I've then chosen from randomly. A few examples of these kinds of targets follow:

Describe the status of Social Security years 2050-2060.

Describe primary transportation between years 2025-2050.

Describe a significant change in civil law for years 2000-2075.

Once these phrases or questions have been written out and placed within envelopes, they are dropped unmarked into a container. The envelopes are all alike (same brand), and can be shuffled by shaking prior to a selection.

When I actually want to do a remote viewing, I randomly select an envelope and put it on top of my computer. I then repeat the following affirmation:

"I will be completely open to whatever information is required to appropriately answer the question contained within the current selected envelope."

An assumption is that the information will be pertinent to the United States, unless the input indicates otherwise. After a few minutes of meditation, I begin to receive the information, which I fill in on the screen of my computer. I write until I am no longer able to do so, or there is no information left to describe. Then I open the envelope and read the actual question or phrase. If the material I have written seems to agree in some way with the question, I save it to the general subject file for which it is a part, then destroy the three-by-five card.

If the information seems to be incomplete, or cannot be understood, but still seems to apply to the question, I save it with a notation that it is not complete and must be read-dressed. I then put the three-by-five card into a fresh envelope and it goes back into the pile.

If nothing agrees or there seems to be any kind of a problem with the information, I delete the information from my screen, and reseal the card in a new envelope, returning it to the container. I always try to maintain a sufficient number of targets within the container to preclude prior knowledge of the subject.

Unfortunately, remote viewing isn't like watching television. Much of the information arrives fractured, that is, somewhat chaotic or in disarray. One then has to try and put it into some kind of an understandable context. How difficult is this? Very. In some cases it almost seems to be impossible. It is this stage in the development of information where everything can go wrong. Sometimes one might be inclined to drift off in a direction that is pure fantasy. Regardless of what anyone tells you, it is nearly impossible to tell when that is happening. The only real way to try and prevent it is to collect enough data to preclude having to jump to too many conclusions—in other words, reduce the leaps of logic required to have the data make sense.

As an example, a targeted envelope may contain the date "mid-2058 C.E.," and the targeting phrase *Describe the primary source of energy in 2075.* The preliminary remote viewer input might read as follows:

"Large cylinder. Flatter on top than bottom. Focused array of some kind. Charged liquid. High-pitched whine. Sequential bursts of light. Swirling heat. Powerful sense of electromagnetic pulsing." Included with the statements may be a drawing or group of drawings relating to one or more of these statements.

Because I know that I am targeting the future, I can't automatically assume that my current concepts of reality will apply in trying to understand what all these statements mean. In other words, what drives the energy system may be some completely new form of science, which is not yet known or understood. Hence, all normal logic breaks down.

Do you abandon the information because you don't understand it? No. You do what you can with it, by retargeting once, twice, or however many times it takes for a concept to evolve, or until a pattern emerges that seems to support the informational fragments.

I've attempted to do this throughout the book. So some of what I've concluded will eventually end up very close to what proves to be true, some of it will gravitate to the opposite end of the stick, or about as far from ground truth as you can imagine. What will be fun is seeing which of it does what. In all cases, it will be fun to read about, and perhaps make for less of a surprise in our future.

Part III

THE NEXT
ONE HUNDRED
YEARS

We can expect a lot to happen over the next fifty to one hundred years. A lot of it will be cyclic—that is, old stuff repeating itself. Some of it will be totally new, or stuff that hasn't happened before. Almost all of it will be interesting.

The way I've decided to lay out this portion of my book is not unique. There is a system, developed by marketing professor Philip Kotler, that is currently being used by business executives in their decision-making processes. Monitoring these categories helps alert them to significant changes within the world of commerce and economics.

It is not a surprise that it is also the system of categories that was chosen by Edward Cornish, president of the World Future Society, to categorize world issues that are addressed within the magazine The Futurist, of which he is the editor.

Since most of my information was collected prior to thinking about how it would be presented, some of the titles for specific categories vary from Kotler's in some areas, but not significantly. For example, where he uses the term "pharmaceuticals," I have used the term "medicine"; another example would be his use of "airplanes" where I use the more general classification of "transportation."

The use of categories also permits the reader to quickly and easily locate an area of interest they might have, without having to wade through the less-interesting stuff.

These categories as I use them are presented in alphabetical order:

Demography	Birth and Death, Children, Ethnic Groups, Marriage, Men & Women, Older Population, Populations, Religious Divisions, Significant Lifestyle Changes, Teens
Economics	Advertising, Banking, Financial
Environmental	Air, Biology, Bridges, Cities, Buildings, Forests, Geology, Highways, Land, Marine, Natural Disasters, Planetary Issues, Weather
Governments	Crime, Diplomacy, Espionage, Ethics, Law, Military, Politics, Taxes, Schools, War (& Peace)
Social	Anthropology, Archaeology, Arts, Education, Entertainment, Families, Holidays, Language, Sex, Sports, General Social
Technology	Computers, Engineering, Medicine, Nuclear Weapons, Power, Spaceships, Telecommunications, Transportation

11

DEMOGRAPHY

Birth and Death

When you start thinking about birth and death, you have to begin with populations. The current world population (mid-1998) is estimated at somewhere very close to six billion people. To understand what that figure actually means, one needs to display it both as total number, as well as a phenomenon of growth. The graph on the following page is based on world population estimates since the first year of the Common Era (C.E.).

It is quickly apparent that with the dawn of the Renaissance and the end of the Middle Ages the human race has grown fruitful and multiplied.

There are a number of reasons why this has occurred, and we can probably attribute most of them to changes in food production, medicine, law, and perhaps transportation.

There are some who see the population slowing down between now and the year 2080 or so. Looking at the current numbers, they have hypothesized that the world's population will actually peak out at only about 10,000 million around the end of the twenty-first century. They base these numbers primarily on the estimated number of years it now takes to add a billion to the overall population, then they figure in an assumed increase in the use of contraceptives by developing countries, and the continuing rise in average ages across the globe.

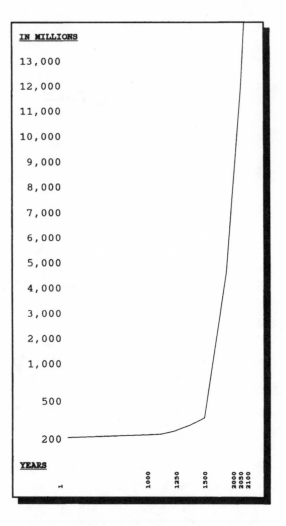

My remote viewings do not support these perceptions. Improvements in living conditions have a way of spurring on child production within developing countries. Also, within developing countries, they require a much larger work force to support their increases in manufacturing and development. Generally, when heads of families feel they can bring home the bacon and provide for a larger family, they will have more children. Increased access to medicine within developing nations will also more than compensate for any improvements in contraception. The only area I've ever seen that truly has a dramatic impact on childbearing is education.

In many areas of the world, the average educational level is rising, but not fast enough to make a difference. In some heavily populated areas of the world, education has recently taken a beating from the reinstitutionalization of archaic religious practices as well as a substantial rise in the continued persecution of women.

Therefore, as early as the year 2050, I predict the world population will already begin to exceed the 10,000 million people mark—easily fifty years ahead of schedule.

Why is this an important figure? It's important because it represents the total number of people we will have a capability to feed. If my remote viewing is correct, our ability to feed the population is actually under stress now. Given our ability to adapt modern technologies and our inventiveness to address such problems, we will probably be able to compensate for these demands for food well into the 9,000 million mark. But, somewhere between the ninth and tenth billion, significant breakdowns in food production will begin to occur. Hence, by the year 2050, food production will be a severe problem.

Many of the industrialized countries, the primary producers of food, will begin to see the handwriting on the wall about the year 2035, but it will essentially be too late to make the changes necessary to prevent wide-scale starvation in many of the still-developing countries. Something will have to be done quickly to thin the ranks.

Since the average population growth, using a straight-line graph, appears to be about 80 million per year (or .08 of one percent), thinning the ranks becomes somewhat more difficult to implement than one might initially think.

There are two ways to do this *thinning out*. There is a hard way—through war—or a more benign or peaceful process—by controlling birth (through attrition).

What about war?

Using history as an example, it would have to be a war to end all wars. Let's assume that we could have a really nasty one, that it's at least twice as bad as either of the two world wars and lasts just about the same amount of time—five to six years.

Assuming the highest possible casualty rate (in deaths), the thinning might look something like the following:

For sake of argument, we'll assume the total number of casualties for military and civilian populations on all sides is somewhere in the neighborhood of 75 million. We could then add in another 125 million to allow for the Hitler, Stalin, and Mao type personalities that always crop up during these times of darkness. This comes to a total of 200 million dead. We could arbitrarily decide that it will probably be at least twice as bad as we can envision it to be, so let's now double our figure to 400 million.

If our population in 2050 is 10,000 million, we can divide our casualty rate (400 million) by this figure, and we can see that the total casualty rate will represent a very small .04 percent in population reduction. If we then figure back in our .8 of one percent (80 million people per year) normal growth rate, we have to add back the 400 million we just lost, which means that we will simply break even.

My conclusion is that we are definitely in big-time trouble.

Is there a peaceful solution? Yes. We have simply to get everyone on the planet to agree to an immediate ten percent reduction in child production beginning right now! By doing so, we could actually slow projected world growth by 500 million people by the year 2050. At the very least, this would give us an additional fifty years to figure out a more permanent solution. Will this happen? You tell me.

Children

Children are the most important commodity walking the face of the planet. Their dreams and aspirations drive the future. What happens over the next 75 to 100 years will be a direct result of not only the decisions we make as adults today, but the visions and accomplishments of our children. Yet child abuse, neglect, and runaways are increasing on almost an exponential basis. This may be in direct correlation to the rise in population, but I doubt it.

When the STARGATE program was exposed and I became publicly known as one of the program's remote viewers, I was nearly overwhelmed with requests to help locate or find missing children. I was absolutely stunned by the fact that while there are numerous organizations that have been set up to look for missing children, there was no real primary or federally funded and supported clearinghouse for maintenance of such files.

I predict that by the end of 2004, the federal government will establish and fund a primary facility to coordinate a nationwide search organization for missing children. It will operate through the Internet and provide local law enforcement and medical facilities with up-to-date and rapid-response information helpful in identifying missing kids.

The point of initiation for this project will be a single grant from an individual estate that will provide the seed monies necessary to design and implement a grass roots drive to address this problem.

In conjunction with this effort, I see a decision by the Supreme Court that acknowledges the "Rights and Laws of Children" as a necessary step toward the reduction of child abuse.

On the down side, with the continuing rise in violence among teens, a decision will be made to bring harsher penalties to children accused of felony crimes. Before the year 2002, the Supreme Court will uphold the conviction of a teen (twelve-to fourteen-years of age) for multiple first-degree murder who will have been tried and sentenced as an adult. This will take place in a Southeastern state—probably Georgia or Florida.

By the year 2010, three new prisons will be constructed, one in the Northeast, one in the South, and one just west of the Rocky Mountains, that will be specifically designed and constructed to house children and teenage offenders between the ages of eleven and sixteen. Modified sentencing will be established that falls somewhere between what an adult might receive and what is currently being levied on teens.

The positive side of this action will be a twenty-year, very intensive study of new methods for behavior modification, which will produce landmark approaches for treating young criminals, rather than punishing them. A key element to this behavior modification will be education (more about this can be found in the section that deals with law.)

Of greater interest to teens, I make the following predictions:

By the year 2010, there will be a complete change in the testing procedures for college entry. The SATs will go the way of the dinosaurs.

By the year 2015, a new method of teaching will be established in most cities, which will differ radically from what is commonly found in most schools today. As an example, most high school students will be able to:

1. Choose the hours they want to attend school.

2. There will be more opportunities to study skill-related subjects such as electronics, information processing, engineering, etc., in the high school environment.

3. There will be a shift back to the old ideas of apprenticeship. A new type of educational system following high school, where "apprentice" and "journeyman" have meaning, will develop. A student will be able to spend four to six years learning a complex or sophisticated professional trade through practical or hands-on application. Surprisingly, this will be driven by the fact that most "high-tech" corporations have to do such training or retraining anyway, and this will be seen as

a way of increasing control over the work force, and a way of reducing educational costs.

The federal and state education administrations will probably duke it out well into the year 2025. The system(s) as they now operate will continue to degenerate to a point that screams for reconstruction. By the year 2015, approximately 60 percent of our children will be attending privatized schools and the public school system will be in shambles. The primary reason for this occurring are the following:

1. By 2015, the administrative costs (at the senior management level) will exceed 50 percent of most school's budgets.

2. Highly qualified teachers will migrate to private institutions in ever-growing numbers.

3. The quality of textbooks, study materials, and library content in most public schools will have been diluted to the point of futility.

4. The battle between community "spiritual" leaders and "nonsectarian" protection groups will have reached a level of near violence.

5. The population of "students" that exists at that time will have been polarized to one of two extremes. Those who have been taught about the power of information, how to access it, how to use it, and those who haven't. Unfortunately, this will be based mostly on social status or social background—a new form of ethnic discrimination.

Action taken by the federal government to make changes within public school systems across the country will require the establishment of martial law in at least six states, much as the enforcement of integration did during the late fifties and early sixties. (See additional information under the specific topic "schools.")

Ethnic Groups

With the coming new millennium, we are changing our view of the planet and how we relate to one another. One of the unique features of our old way of relating is that our tribal distinctions, that is, what makes us different from our neighbors, had significant meaning. Tribal differences don't just occur between tribes of people. Sometimes they can happen on a block-to-block or street-to-street basis within neighborhoods, as well as along distinctive borders between countries, or within them.

To get a mental picture of what is going on, think of these tribal differences, or pockets of identification, as being well-defined sections of Earth, small continents floating on the surface of a globe. Where they make no contact there is no problem. Where they do, we have earthquakes.

In the past, there was plenty of room for these small continents to float around. There was even room within the borders of single continents for individual landmasses to shift or move. Sometimes there were both accidental as well as deliberate "bumps" between masses, which usually resulted in earthquakes. The size of the quake was usually dependent on how accidental or deliberate the "bump" might have been. In some cases it might have had more to do with pressure building up over time, sort of like two land masses resting against one another with neither wanting to give space to the other. Well, we are quickly running out of space, so the number of "bumps" and the degree to which they quake, are going to climb exponentially. This will especially be true where there is little give—within country borders (dictatorships), and between countries (where there is least agreement or compatibility).

There is a good side to this. Just as the movement of mountains and the creation or destruction of land on a planetary scale is inevitable, so is the requirement for change unavoidable. Knowing this, we simply have to acquiesce to the requirement.

Notice I did not say it would be easy. What I mean by this is that knowing it is going to happen and that it is unavoidable, we should be willing to negotiate how it's going to happen before it becomes a forced situation.

A good example of nonnegotiation would be what is now called ethnic cleansing! A highly charged phrase that, truth be known, was probably originally coined by and designed to sell newspapers. However, as distasteful as it may be, it represents something that is very real and very dangerous.

Within Bosnia, Serbia, and Croatia, parts of what used to be southwestern Russia, segments of Africa, inside Iraq, and a number of other countries, this is already happening. In some of these places, it has to do with tribal differences that go back hundreds of years. Others are religion based, and some center on political zeal, or simply deal with old vendettas and revenge.

Generally, we are not talking about greed or power here, but clashes stemming from differences in ethnic belief, or out of some ethnic idealism. These types of clashes are not going to go away. They will only increase.

For whatever reasons, areas within which we can expect major clashes and their specific periods include the following:

2010-2015 C.E. There will be significant problems at the border areas of the United States and Mexico—specifically San Diego/Tijuana, and Juarez/El Paso. As a result, Mexico and the United States will enter into an open border treaty that will go into effect in conjunction with a similar Canadian/American treaty sometime near 2020-2022 C.E. The opening for this treaty will occur when all three countries have agreed to a common effort toward adopting both a common currency as well as equalization of workers/unions rights/benefits. The agreement will be initiated, but full commonality will not take place until approximately 2030-2035 C.E.

2018-2020 C.E. There will be a small border clash between Peru, Colombia, and Brazil over disputed land areas that have direct access to the Amazon River. This will be settled by international treaty and by the direct intervention of Venezuela and Chilean diplomats.

2009-2011 C.E. Border clashes between Gambia and Senegal, Sierra Leone and Liberia, the Congo and Central African Republic will erupt over land disputes. They will last for a period of two, one, and four years, respectively.

2006-2008 C.E. Algeria will take exception to border issues with Tunisia, which will invite the intervention of Libya into both their affairs by the year 2010 C.E. Efforts to solve this dilemma will fail for a period of nearly fifteen years, during which it will spread to civil unrest within Libya, eventually erupting into civil war. (See section on war.)

2009-2010 C.E. There will be a minor clash between Namibia and Botswana over the Caprivi Zipfel area, which will be resolved peacefully between them. However, Angola will take exception to the agreement, sparking some sporadic unrest within the area for a short period.

2006-2008 C.E. There will be a major clash between the countries of Zaire and Zambia over tribal-held lands that currently divide them. This problem will surface when one of the smaller, currently less vocal tribal elements shifts political sides following the death of one of their senior statesmen. This problem will be solved in the old-fashioned way—through marriage.

Present-2035 C.E. There will be continual clashes, from moderate to severe, that will occur in the region presently occupied by Georgia, Azerbaijan, Armenia, Iran, and extreme southwest Russia. (See section on war.)

2009-2012 C.E. Problems will erupt initially between the governments of Afghanistan and Tadzhikistan, and will quickly spread first to Uzbekistan, then extreme northern Pakistan. By 2012 C.E., the Himachal Pradesh and Punjab areas of extreme northern India will be involved. (This will probably not be a military problem, but it will certainly involve substantial civilian unrest throughout these regions.)

2000-2100 C.E. There will be continual minor flashes of conflict on borders separating Cambodia, Laos, Myanmar, Thailand, Vietnam, as well as their shared borders with China. Most of these clashes will be at the instigation of local warlords within the nearly inaccessible mountain regions. Toward the end of this hundred-year period, they will taper off to none, and there will probably be a reestablishment of more permanent border lines between Laos, Vietnam, and Cambodia based on natural terrain features. The islands currently under dispute between China and Vietnam will be relinquished to Vietnam in exchange for concessions in fishing in the Gulf of Tonkin.

2000-2005 C.E. Russia and Japan will settle their disputes over islands due east of Hokkaido.

2025-2026 C.E. Malaysia will absorb the state of Brunei.

2010-2012 C.E. Islands north of the Torres Strait will be deeded by Australia to Papua New Guinea (Saibai, Boigu, Talbot, Turnagain islands and Warrior reefs.)

The important message here is that people of the world, regardless of tribal affiliation, will have to begin to recognize that retaining such tribal affiliations and protecting the tribal culture is OK, but it cannot be done at the expense someone else. There is room for intercultural respect, and by showing such, one is not selling out a religious or political belief. In fact, if such cooperation and respect does not develop, then our planet is doomed to eventual destruction from within.

Marriage

I've developed a unique perception about marriage through the years of remote viewing. It has come from having so many couples asking for help in one way or another. What they asked for usually had nothing to do with their relationship. It was more day-to-day stuff like asking for help in deciding how they were going to pay a mortgage, or what they should do with the proceeds from the sale of their company, or maybe something even simpler, like where to put the garden next to their house, or where did my wife lose her ring. But it was unavoidable that I would get some degree of insight into their current or ongoing relationship(s).

What did I see there?

It wasn't so much the individual couples who provided insight into marriage, but over the years, it was the summation of their input. When you get something from a few couples it might not be correct, but when you pick it up from many, you can say that it might be true.

Local television, newspapers, magazines, books, periodicals, church publications, polls, questionnaires, textbooks, etc., have all been hammering about how marriages are going down the tubes at a rapidly increasing rate. Divorce rates are going up as we speak, and the sudden great influx in broken homes is very threatening.

But . . . my sense of these things, is that none of this is really true. Yes, divorce rates are climbing, but marriages are not failing as miserably as one would think. The two figures do not mean the same thing.

We live in times when information has become the new commodity. There are polls for everything. And because there are polls, we have developed a whole system of definitions that are very black and white and have well-defined edges dividing them one from the other. It's always a multiple choice, and we have to always check this or check that in a column.

As an example, circle the following:

Married: YES   NO

Divorced: YES   NO

Circling NO under married and YES under divorced implies that one has not been living with someone very happily for twenty-five years, which may not be applicable to a number of couples I know.

Circling YES to married and NO to divorced implies that someone is happily married, when they may have been living separate for many years. Again, this is a very large assumption.

My experience has been that when it comes to relationships, one cannot assume without asking some very specific questions. I've known people who have been living together for longer than thirty years but who were never married. In another case, I've known a very dear couple who has been living happily together for twenty-two years. Both have been married the entire time, but neither to each other. Before you run off on a tangent, I must add that they are of opposite sex.

But, then there are same-sex couples who have lived together for a very long period of time as well, who of course are not married. Not because they don't want to be, but simply because someone's or some group's view of morality dictates they should not be. In reference to at least two of these cases, the relationship between these couples has lasted longer than anyone I know that is married to the opposite sex. One couple is male; the other is female.

I know of some couples who have been divorced a number of times, but almost immediately and continuously remarry. Do we total the number of years they are married, or do we total the divorces and give more weight to them? I myself have been divorced twice and married three times. My total number of married years since age twenty-one is twenty-seven. The total number of years I have been unmarried are four. My longest marriage of course, my last one, is the current one. We have been happily married for a period of nearly fourteen years, and I hope another fourteen. My first wife remarried, and as far as I know still happily is. My second wife was also looking to remarry the last I heard. My point is that this figure that no one ever looks at is important when you start evaluating the vows of matrimony. Just because some go wrong once or twice, doesn't mean they aren't wedded to the idea.

Having spent some time remote viewing a number of cultures, across a number of historical periods, I have concluded that the way in which we look at marriage needs to be fully reevaluated. Our current rules don't make any sense. They are designed to follow not what works but what our current religious and political dogmas dictate, even when these dogmas go against the grain. Because these dogmas change from culture to culture on a decade-to-decade basis, they are arbitrary, and probably cause more problems than they are worth. They are certainly less functional. We have only to look at the currently ending millennium for some very good examples of why things should change.

It wasn't too long ago that a man could be married to as many women as he wished (in fact there are still some states and countries that allow this.) There may or may not be anything wrong with this. But shouldn't the rule apply both ways? A woman can't be married to as many men as she would like to be. Why not?

Not too long ago a man could divorce his wife by throwing her out the front door and denouncing her in public four times. He got to keep the kids, the house, the wares. Now the man drags his own suitcase out through the front door and the wife gets the kids along with the house in most states.

Before some of my female readers jump with joy, remember that in some very large and supposedly modern countries, the woman can still be thrown through the door and denounced four times. Scary as it might seem, in some cases they can even be murdered in view of witnesses and without recourse.

At one time, there were no rules about the minimum age at which one could marry, a custom that still exists in four or five countries. Guess who made up that rule? Also, there are still countries that make very little distinction between marriage and slavery. The wife is chattel, is kept absolutely ignorant, subservient, and in some cases is beaten on a regular basis—usually in the name of religion. I think the same group of guys made that rule up as well. The scary part here is that when you talk to some of the women who live under those conditions, they will tell you how honored they are.

Popes used to be married . . . oops, pardon me, they only lived their lives with a woman, they were never *officially* married. However, they were viewed as married enough that their sons could assume their estates and power after they died. In some cases, those estates included huge amounts of church property.

Before all you Protestants walk off shaking your heads and *tsking* at the Catholics, you might look at some of the brutality carried into marriage by some of your early church leaders. Women and children alike suffered abominably under the pendant of religion—nearly all religions. In some countries today they still suffer for those very same reasons.

At one time kings changed their wives like clothing, some still do. When divorce was viewed as OK, the women got to live out their days in a convent somewhere (God forbid they try to remarry, like the king), and when it wasn't OK, they simply lost their heads or took a short fall out of a castle window.

So, when we begin to address marriage, we have to take into account the period we are referencing, then we have to be very careful not to date the material. I believe it's easier doing a metanalysis on the paranormal than it would be to do one on the sacred act of marriage.

Looking at today, I believe we are standing on a threshold in history that may actually be the doorway to the fairest period of all, at least when it comes to marriage. Now if only we can shuck the final remnants of hair shirt that seem to cling to the process.

In light of the above, by the year 2025 C.E., marriage will finally be recognized as any union between two human beings, under the following conditions:

1. Where one human being voluntarily lives with another human being, for the sake of sharing in all of life's hardships and benefits, they will be considered married.

2. Where one human being dies while under the day-to-day care of another human being, to whom they are not related by blood (an officially recognized act of unconditional love), they will be considered married.

3. Where two human beings share in the difficulties of protecting, providing for, and raising a family—children (whether their kids or someone else's won't matter), they will be considered married.

There will be addendums, of course. A few of these will be as follows:

1. Sex won't be a mediating factor—neither the sex of the individuals involved, or the fact they might be or might not be having any. If they are having sex, with whom won't matter.

2. Marriage will not require a religious or political blessing. NOTE: I said it won't *require* one. Having one will still be thought of as a nice confirmation of their vows to one another.

3. While residing as a couple under contract of marriage, all matters of support, such as taxes, responsibilities, bills, ownership, etc., will be equally shared.

4. All matters of support, such as taxes, responsibilities, bills, ownership, etc., that are brought into the marriage as individuals will remain individually held.

5. Divorce will be supervised by courts and no longer

affected by lawyers. In other words, the rules won't change from case to case, or be based on income.

While this will probably be something very close to the rule within the United States, and some of the Western European countries, it will not be prevalent throughout the world. In fact, by 2025 C.E., women's rights in a number of countries, such as parts of Africa and the Middle East, will have reverted to their more primitive concepts.

Women's rights will become a hot topic within the United Nations by 2008-2010 C.E. These issues will help to usher in a growing conflict within many of those regions of the world (see section on war.) The only way these "customs" will be altered will be through outside intervention.

Men and Women

By 2005-2008 C.E., changes in the attitudes and lifestyles of men and women will change—perhaps not radically but distinctively. By the end of that three-year period, a new form of clothing style will be ushered in. It will be called "utilitarian."

Basically, it will be a new clothing design genre, consisting of a more androgynous look. This will begin with a form of jumpsuit, not unlike something you would have seen on *Star Trek* twenty-five years ago. The only differences between men and women in these designs will be the color or piping that covers the shoulders. Initially, colors will be fairly bright and different, however these will quickly give way to moderation.

By 2015 C.E., hairstyles will become more and more similar. Men and women alike will begin to share the same styling when it comes to their locks.

For men, dyeing the hair will become more prevalent, as well as having the hair cut in layers. We will begin to see men with streaks of color in their hair, as well as decorative touches like glitter and the like. Initially this will be happening in places of recreation, like dance bars, discos, or nightclubs.

Women will begin to wear their hair in much shorter cuts. Some women will even prefer to go bald, at least partially, beginning with the shaving of the sides, and progressing to fully shaved heads. Of course, those who do will be sporting some rather unique and decorative tattoos on their craniums (both permanent and nonpermanent).

By 2005 C.E. tattoos will be fully back in vogue, but they won't be permanent. New dyes will be developed that will be impervious to water or other fluids, even sweat. The only way to remove these tattoos will be with oils specifically designed to loosen them. Initially, women will wear more tattoos than men will.

Tattoos will be a means of sharing something about ourselves with those we meet—the automatic or unspoken word. Some tattoos will be highly erotic, while others will make very loud statements concerning mental state. By the year 2020 C.E., there will be almost as many tattoo parlors (for temporary tattoo design and application) as there are nail/hair parlors today. The single greatest use of the temporary tattoo will be to emulate clothing not actually being worn.

By 2020 C.E., an entirely new scent business will have come into being. Rather than designing aftershave for men and perfume for women based on odors, these new companies will be designing "scents" based on pheromones.

Pher-o-mone /'fer-a-mon/ n [ISV phero- (fr. Greek pherein to carry) + -mone (as in hormone)]—a chemical substance that is produced by an animal and serves esp. as a stimulus to other individuals of the same species for one or more behavioral responses—pher-o-mon-al /'fer-a-mo-n'l/ adj (Merriam Webster's Collegiate Dictionary, Tenth Edition).

Worn on the skin, these pheromones will essentially key off specific responses in men and women when they meet. These responses will range from sexual arousal to the desire to eat. In some cases, they will make the person objectionable—being worn like the scent of a guard dog.

A secondary business will stem from the first, in which scents will be developed to neutralize the originals—so that one may walk among the living without being manipulated. If you think this sounds far-fetched, I will tell you that by the year 2025 C.E. some of the scents that will have been developed will have such power that they will be legally outlawed or at least forbidden to minors.

Pheromones will also be used as part of the behavior-modification techniques utilized in criminal rehabilitation. (See the sections on crime and law.)

By the year 2020 C.E., a new form of jewelry will be available. It will be much like the old "mood ring" that everyone remembers from the 1960s. However, in this case, it will cover a greater portion of the body. Upper sections of skintight jumpsuits will actually change color across the spectrum based on the emotional condition of the wearer. For those less inclined to the risqué, decorative armband-type bracelets, necklaces, and scarves will come in a multitude of colors that will shift spectrums dependent on the wearer's mood.

As fallout from military developments, by the year 2015 C.E., we will begin to see segments of clothing and jewelry that will mimic their surroundings, chameleon-like. If a person is standing against a neon background in a nightclub, his or her jewelry and segments of clothing will mimic this—changing and jumping from background element to background element.

Older Population

What will the older population think about all this? I can only speak for myself. It'll be great.

By 2029-2030 C.E., we will have access to whole new categories of chemicals and materials genetically based in origin.

One of these *enzymes* will operate something like the trigger mechanism in the cells of trees found in northern climates. Injected, it will actually seek out cells involved in wrinkles, causing them to reinfuse with fluids, thereby eliminating those unsightly lines. Initially this will only work on the crow's-feet around the eyes and with lip lines. But with time, people will at least appear to age much more slowly.

Sometime very soon, perhaps as early as 2002 C.E., male-pattern baldness will be fully eradicated. Men will be able to control this problem with pills. This will be unveiled by the same company that currently produces a semieffective cream. (Something similar to this was announced in television commercials sometime during the first or second week in May, approximately nine months after I made this prediction. I've left this in, since I've been unable to verify specifically whether or not it is the same as what I have predicted.)

By 2009-2010 C.E., recreation for the aged will finally be taken seriously. Many of the now-operating health spas, workout clubs, and gyms that cater to the middle-aged and younger will convert to "Senior Clubs." These clubs will organize and manage recreational packages specifically designed for and catering to the more mature.

Most of them will offer assistance with "coupling" or "friendship bonding," as it will be called by then. It will be a very sophisticated and computerized matching or mating system for essentially one-night stands.

For those who feel this is morally objectionable, there will be just as many operating under the banner of the local church, as not. For by the year 2006 C.E., the single greatest recognized disease (dis-ease) of the aged will be loneliness! It will be viewed as the number-one killer. All of our formal organizations, including churches, insurance organizations, hospitals, etc., which by then will be getting most of their funding from the more mature, will be addressing this as an issue.

By the year 2015 C.E., most will acknowledge quality of life as more important than length of life, thus putting a whole new outlook on life that will reverberate throughout culture.

By 2010 C.E., there will be a new drug for improving

sexual activity well into the seventies. Hotels, motels, and vacation packages will be specifically designed to entice the older lovers through their doors. This will be somewhat accelerated by 2020 C.E., following development of the new pheromone scents previously discussed.

A more serious problem to the older population will center on consumption. By 2006-2008 C.E., the numbers of older citizens (those above the age of sixty-five) will rise significantly, and continue to rise for at least a seven- to eight-year period. The proportion of money being spent by the elderly versus the younger generation will begin to polarize the overall population on specific issues centering on consumption.

Notice I said "being spent" above. Issues surrounding services or support through government-controlled agencies will still be coming primarily from taxes. These are areas primarily supported by taxing the young.

The younger generations will suddenly find that many of these services are being driven primarily by the old; subsequently many of these programs will be costing the young more than they might be willing to provide.

This issue will have to be addressed. So, by the year 2015 C.E., a commission will be set up to address some of these grievances. Since the commission will primarily consist of the elderly, further polarization will occur, eventually resulting in a minor revolution within the below age forty-five population.

As a result, there will be a number of significant changes in how we currently view major issues within our culture. Some of these include the following:

1. By 2020 C.E., stringent guidelines will come into being that begin to restrict medical services that prolong life or their availability. These services will no longer be provided simply because they are available. They will only be provided when there can be assurances that the quality of life will be present as well. Who will make these judgments? Like it or not, in some cases the courts will have to

make these decisions. However, most will be made by families, and these decisions will be supported by the elderly in most cases.

2. By 2020 C.E., assisted suicide will become a lawful choice. There will even be a government program that helps alleviate the burden on insurance companies, which will be required to pay off on life insurance policies for those who chose suicide over a prolonged illness. As much as some organized religions will balk at this, it is inevitable. In fact, it will be the creation of new religious organizations and modification of older organizations that will be the primary supporters of these new policies. This will require at least two significant and landmark decisions by the U.S. Supreme Court prior to the year 2016 C.E.

3. Tax considerations for people who care and provide for members of the older generation will be considerably broader. They will be expanded to at least an equal footing with the considerations for the care and raising of children. By the year 2009 C.E., we will see new "older brother/older sister" organizations being formed, where there will be dual mentoring between the old and the young. Young people will be allowed to adopt older individuals, much as they adopt children today. By 2015 C.E., there will be agencies handling these adoptions.

And of course, everyone is interested in what is going to happen to Social Security. If I simply said it doesn't exist in the year 2025 C.E., this would probably instill panic within many. So I will try and describe what I see in a little more detail.

By the year 2010 C.E., at least 50 percent of the current

social security system will be supported privately. By 2020 C.E., it will cease to exist as we currently understand it.

Citizens, civil employers, state, and federal governments will still have to invest in programs for the future support of the elderly, but these programs will have been privatized as "for profit" investment firms.

These firms will be heavily monitored and governed by strict state and federal laws, but essentially they will be motivated and oriented toward profit making. What will be unique about them is the fact that no one firm will be isolated from another. Excessive profits by one will be shared with the others, and excessive losses by one will also be shared with the others. Each firm will be oriented toward different investment strategies and their employees will be hired or fired based on their ability to effect positive or negative results.

Citizens will have the choice as to which firm they can belong, some being more high risk than others. The amount of return at time of retirement will be based on a minimum to a maximum investment over time. Of course, those who invest more can expect more. Those who invest the minimum will receive the minimum, but it will be possible to invest less at higher risk and thereby make more as a result. That should appease the hidden gambler in those who want more control.

The greatest enticement to support this changeover from the current system to the new will be generated by how the process is controlled—that is, who actually says where the money will go, or what will be done with it. By 2020 C.E., investment decisions will be made by the citizen(s) through direct links such as the Internet.

These changes will not be without problems. The system will require at least two significant governmental patches (single allotments of funds from the overall budget) to survive past its development stage. One will take place about 2012 C.E., the second about 2018 C.E.

Populations

Within the next one hundred years, the single greatest population growth will take place in Asia, followed by Africa, North/South America, then Europe (primarily Central Europe.) While the population will nearly double in Asia and Africa, it will rise significantly less in North America and Europe. South America will rise by at least a third.

There are extremes that occur within populations. One might look at them as spikes in a graph. I've listed the top three of these spikes under each major topic or heading on the following charts. These are generalizations to show where activity will probably be spiking at quarter points over the next one hundred years.

A number of other areas are primarily covered more exclusively under specific topic titles in other areas of this book.

Most of these graphic spikes do not occur exactly on the dates listed, but fall within a few years one way or the other. The important thing to remember is that these are gross generalizations and there will be variances within the primary groups. Saying the unemployment will be extremely high or spiking in Southeast Asia in 2025 may not mean in all countries. The economy might be booming in Vietnam during that time period, while being on the average significantly worse in other Southeast Asian countries. So, these are intended to be general guides.

Major Heading	Year	Area
Unemployment	2025	Southeast Asia (includes Japan)
	2050	South America
	2075	Western Europe
Loss of Cultures	2025	Brazil, India, Africa
	2050	Pacific Peoples
	2075	Central Asia
Highest Rate of Suicide	2025	Northern Europe
	2050	Central China
	2075	Central Europe
Greatest Increase in Military Spending	2025	Middle East
	2050	Central Europe
	2075	China
Significant Change in Political System	2025	Middle East
	2050	Africa
	2075	North America
Most Disastrous Economy	2025	Central Europe
	2050	Central Asia
	2075	South America
Best Economy	2025	Western Europe
	2050	Southeast Asia
	2075	North America
Highest Rate of Inflation	2025	Central Asia
	2050	South America
	2075	Central Asia
Highest Consumption of Energy (Fuel Oil)	2025	North America
	2050	South America
	2075	Western Europe
Highest Consumption of Energy (Natural Gas)	2025	North America
	2050	North America
	2075	North America
Highest Consumption of Energy (Coal)	2025	Western Europe
	2050	Far East
	2075	China
Highest Consumption of Energy (Electricity)	2025	North America
	2050	North America
	2075	Western Europe

Major Heading	Year	Area
Highest Consumption of Energy (Nuclear)	2025	North America
	2050	Western Europe
	2075	Far East
Highest Consumption of Energy (Hydroelectric)	2025	North America
	2050	China
	2075	China
Greatest Exporter of Natural Resources	2025	North America
	2050	Central Europe
	2075	Central Europe
Greatest Exporter of Manufactured Goods	2025	South East Asia
	2050	China
	2075	China
Greatest Exporter of Technology	2025	North America
	2050	Western Europe
	2075	Central Europe
Greatest Exporter of Information	2025	North America
	2050	North America
	2075	North America

Religious Divisions

The major divisions in modern religions are considered to be Baha'ism, Buddhism, Christianity, Confucianism, Hinduism, Islam (Muslim), Jainism, Judaism, Sikhism, Shintoism, and Taoism. These are further divided into twenty-four subdenominations: Christianity having the most, ten; followed by Hinduism with three; and Islam with four. There are a lot of other religions still being practiced. However, those above comprise nearly 96 percent of the world's devout.

I have not listed atheism, since I do not consider, nor do I believe the atheists consider, this to be a religion. I likewise totally reject the dictionary definition for atheism, since it makes a generalized morality judgment that suggests that godlessness is in some way evil or wicked. I've know some very moral and righteous atheists in my life who in some cases were far kinder and gentler than many who would consider themselves devout.

In numbers, the major religions look something like the following:

Religion	Number(est.)	Percentage of Total
Christianity	2,200.9 million	43.
Islam (Muslim)	1,250.6 million	24.2
Hinduism	900.0 million	17.6
Buddhism	400.5 million	7.8
Taoism	228.2 million	.045
Sikhism	22.0 million	.0042
Judaism	21.4 million	.0041
Confucianism	7.4 million	.0014
Baha'ism	6.0 million	.0012
Jainism	4.5 million	.00087
Shintoism	4.1 million	.0008
(other)	75.1 million	.0146

By the year 2025, there will be a significant drop in the number of Christians. The actions precipitating this overall reduction are the following:

1. Radical polarization. Many of the denominations currently operating will either soften their dogmatic views or harden them to the point that long-term practitioners will begin to abandon ship. These people will gravitate to smaller, more radical, and unforgiving sects, or change their beliefs entirely. The primary groups that will lose membership are the Roman Catholics, Baptists, and Lutherans. About half of those

lost will actually leave the Christian faith, while about half will move to other denominations, producing a surge in Pentecostal and Church of Christ memberships.

2. There will be a greater influx and acceptance of the Middle Eastern and Eastern religions within the Western world. By 2025, we will see a rise in North American Buddhism, Islam, and Taoism.

3. There will be a significant rise in new religious denominations that are not yet apparent.

4. There will be a significant rise in atheism.

The primary growth in Islam will occur within the Sufi and Sunni denominations. Their call to peaceful resolution of differences will be attractive to those in much of Africa who have not yet been converted, as well to those in the West who want a closer and more disciplined connection to God, but at the same time want to retain their conservative public viewpoints.

Sometime between 2015 and 2022, there will be significant clashes between the Sunni and Shi'a denominations of Islam within the Middle East. This conflict will be centered in the area of Afghanistan, southern Central Russia, and Iran. It will come to a peaceful resolution, but only after three powerful or key mullahs have passed from the planet—one in Iran, and two in Afghanistan.

The single greatest growth in religion will be in Taoism; when China relaxes governmental control between 2008 and 2009, Taoism will sweep their nation. While Christianity will see some improvement within China at the same time, it will always be viewed as a politically threatening tool of the West and under harsh, strict control within China.

Within North America, the Mormon, Presbyterian, and Lutheran church denominations will continue to wane throughout the next hundred years.

Beginning sometime between 2002 and 2005, there will be a concerted effort to birth a new view of religion that is designed to bring religion and science together again, but without the emphasis on Christianity. Its primary dogma will be based on universal rules or laws of the spirit. These new religious principals will attempt to merge current scientific belief with current spiritual thinking. This new religion will address the ephemeral science of soul, or how man's interaction with reality affects life, health, and well-being. It may even be called something like The Metaphysical Church of Science. This will be a rough birth initially, as it will be seen as threatening in the extreme. However, in its design, it will allow for individual variations of belief, and preach respect for those individual variances. By the year 2050, it will have established a firm base in both alternative healing practices as well as in comforting the dying or distressed.

The sign for this church will be the *Infinity Symbol*, superimposed on a circle:

Rather than be threatened by this, other denominations should take warning from this prediction and begin now to expand on the issues surrounding unconditional love, as well as the need to integrate the morality of science into their dogma.

The current pope will die late in the year of 1999. The new pope will be Italian (but not a native Italian), and take the name of Pius XIII.

The Catholic Church will allow its priests to marry by the year 2020. Monks, brothers, and nuns will continue to be required to remain unmarried and celibate at least until

2035, when a few of the organizations will fall to pressure from outside as well as within.

By the year 2005, women will be allowed to participate in the Catholic Mass ceremony, but only within North American and Western European churches.

Sometime between the years 2011 and 2013, additional Dead Sea Scrolls will be located. One will refer directly to the writings of John; the other will make references to holy days as referred to by the Hebrew Bible (Old Testament).

Significant Lifestyle Changes

By 2015, the four-day workweek will be commonplace. People will choose when they begin their week and when they end it, with some going to work Sunday through Wednesday, and some Tuesday through Friday. Families with very young children will follow a schedule like Saturday through Tuesday for the father, and Tuesday through Friday for the mother—requiring a sitter or day school for only one day—Tuesday. People without young children will select days that help reduce traffic to and from work.

Sometime between 2004 and 2006, a new movement will be birthed that is targeted toward the elimination of television watching. As unlikely as it might sound, Parents against Television (PAT) will gain a great following within two or three years, preferring the sharing of activities with their kids rather than the boob tube. Unfortunately, peer pressure in the schools and from the workplace will doom this effort and this movement will probably collapse sometime around 2010 or 2011.

With regard to television, a new "major network" will emerge prior to the year 2005. It will be based on the introduction of new technology that transmits a signal at least three times higher quality (in pixels) than is currently seen on American televisions. The screen required for watching this channel will be wider than it is in height and a minimum of forty-four inches in diagonal. This is also the technology that will replace all other forms of information transfer using computers—at least for a short (five-year) period.

In the year 2008, a cable channel will be added that only broadcasts high-quality animations of the top comic books. Contrary to what we would like to believe, this cable program will air late at night as an adult feature not meant for children, because of its risqué content, which will be primarily sexual in nature. This cable program will be supported by foreign money.

Housing in America will slowly begin to reduce in square footage beginning in the new millennium (year 2000). By the year 2020, the average house with two adults and two kids will not exceed 1250 square feet, have no basement, and will probably be at least a quadriplex (interconnected four-house unit.)

Cooking a full meal will have gone the way of the dinosaur by the year 2025. All meals will be prepackaged and frozen, cooked instantly by microwave. Prepared meals will only be attempted for very special occasions: e.g., birthdays, anniversaries, Easter, Christmas, Thanksgiving, etc., and will cost an excessive amount of money. By 2050, specialty stores will exist that cater to clients who still feel a need to cook individual entrées for meals. You will have to have a very good income to splurge on this type of meal. By 2025, almost all food production will be targeted toward restaurants and prepackaged meal manufacturers.

Restaurants will continue to expand in numbers through the year 2012. Following a rash of food-production disasters, they will begin to fail (further information on this is in the section on food production.) By the year 2025, nearly half the existent restaurants at the change of the millennium will have disappeared. To eat a meal in even the cheapest of restaurants will require making reservations weeks in advance, and they will be excessively expensive. Indeed, the only reason restaurants will exist by the year 2050 is for vanity purposes.

Teens

No surprise here. Teenagers will be just as unique and difficult as they have ever been. The difference will be that they will have to carry a lot more responsibility. The dividing line between teenager and adult will be even more waffled by the year 2010.

Accidental pregnancy will cease to exist by the year 2050. Teenagers will be immunized against accidental pregnancy on a year-to-year basis. Those who fail to be immunized will have their pregnancies aborted, or the fetus will be removed and transferred to otherwise barren mothers. While this might sound very draconian to some, it will grow out of a very logical chain of events and seem to be a simple solution by the time these events come to pass.

Teens will be wearing tracking devices by 2020. However, using these devices to track kids by parents will be unlawful. These devices will be encrypted and will be only for the use of law enforcement to locate missing children (runaways) and kidnap victims. These tracking devices will be subcutaneously inserted somewhere on the body and activated by pressure. Tracking support will be provided by new technology mounted on cell-phone towers, and operated transparent to normal cell-phone operations. This same technology can be used to track cell-phones and beepers.

Teenage driver's licenses will be restricted to certain kinds of vehicles by the year 2025. These vehicles will have upper limits in horsepower and require certain safety features other automobiles will not require: automatic safety harnesses, side and front air bags, additional body strengthening, and armored floor-to-ceiling integral seats. Requirements for the operation of these cars will run with learner permits (ages fourteen through sixteen) and high school ages (seventeen to eighteen years.) The single driving force behind these requirements will be automobile insurance companies and a significant and steady rise in drunk driving deaths for teenagers over a five-year period, 2020 through 2025.

Military service will be officially recognized as an alternative to legal punishment for teenage felons between the ages of eighteen and twenty, very soon after the change to the new millennium—perhaps by the year 2002. None of the services will like this idea, but it will be initiated through an agreement between the Senate Arms Committee and a special committee formed specifically to address teenage crime within the Senate (in the year 1999-2000).

A bill authorizing a teenager's "Right to Work" will be passed in the year 2000, lowering the normal hiring age to fourteen. However, teenagers between the ages of fourteen and eighteen will be restricted to a less than twenty-hour workweek and to occupations that are not considered to be dangerous or that might expose a teenager to toxic chemicals. This bill will be extinguished by the year 2050.

Attempts to make teenagers liable as adults for their behavior will fail through 2022. Legislation will be passed, however, in 2023, that will ensure that teens serve the same sentence as adults for specific crimes. Surprisingly, the types of crimes driving this campaign will not be crimes like murder or assault, but instead will be crimes like grand theft auto, and destruction of private property, and most of these crimes will be gang related.

By the year 2015, antigang legislation will be passed that makes it illegal for more than three teenagers to congregate on the streets. As part of a behavior modification program, members of the same gang will be required to wear tracking bracelets that automatically signal proximity to like signals (bracelets being worn by other gang members.) For other predictions concerning teens, please refer back to my section on children.

12

ECONOMICS

Advertising

This is an area of interest that I would probably rate some-where beneath the topic of war or pestilence. One thing I learned in targeting this subject area is that when it comes to advertising, at one time or another, we have all been victims.

One of the most insidious forms of advertising is the "buy XXXX because XXXX provides something more than our competitor brand YYYY does." Then of course YYYY adver-tises that they do something else better than the XXXX product does because of their secret ingredient.

You as a consumer become involved in taking sides, whether you want to or not. You find yourself standing in the store trying to determine, not only which is better, but if you *need* more of that extra ingredient in XXXX or more of that secret ingredient in YYYY.

What you don't know, and would be utterly surprised by, is that these two apparently hard-core competitors, XXXX and YYYY, are actually owned by the same consortium of individu-als in the first place, that XXXX and YYYY are essentially the same, and the whole idea was to make you feel like you needed one or the other, whether you did or you didn't. There are at least six companies I know of that are presently doing this. I won't name them here, because I can't afford the lawsuit.

Numerous companies are and have been using sublimi-nals for advertising purposes. One of the difficulties in addressing this as a problem is a lack of understanding of what "subliminal influence" means. One of the myths is that it operates something like a quick frame inserted within the ad that says something like "You have to go out and buy XXXX now!" This could not be farther from the truth. Attempts to utilize such crude methods would be doomed to failure. This is not how subliminal influence operates.

Let's say that I have a new kind of snack food that I want people to buy. It basically consists of dough in the form of a cakelike circle, covered with a very general tomato sauce, and some kind of meat like ground beef, all tacked together with cheese—pretty simple and very cheap to manufacture, certainly nothing special.

The first thing I do is a survey to find out what the latest teenage buzzword is for snack food. Let's assume it's "munchies." So I call this new product "Munch'ets—The power snack." I then hire some people to find out what kind of music teenagers like to listen to when they are snacking. I bring this into my advertising background. I might study a couple of hundred kids so that I can understand what keys off hunger. Maybe hunger is predominantly keyed off by the color red. I now have my wrapper. I also notice kids are clock watchers, the closer they get to six o'clock, the more they listen for the dinner bell. So on goes a picture of a clock face that reads ten minutes to six.

By the time this snack food hits the streets, I've got a firm handle on at least seven or eight major buttons that motivate teenagers to eat something. It is no surprise that they now begin to pester their parents to pick this new snack food up the next time they go to the store.

Even better, I might use some subtle technique that influences the parents to buy it as a means for "making their kids happy and more appreciative of their parents." Talk about subtle.

But that isn't all. Having embedded very subliminal messages within the wrapping, color, music, and pictures, I now add the coup de grace—fear. If your kids don't eat this, they are not getting some essential vitamin that makes them smarter, faster, or more energetic than any of the others. Fear alone will nearly double sales of most products.

How many times have you heard phrases like "more doctors choose," or "highly recommended by family physicians"? Don't think about the product, but simply stop for a moment and think about what these phrases actually mean to you, what effect they might be having on you emotionally. Then consider how many times a day you hear them, or phrases like them.

I'm not implying that advertisers are doing anything wrong by using such techniques to get us to buy something. What I am saying is that we are bombarded by these things on an hour-to-hour, minute-to-minute basis, through the media, visually and auditorially. We live our day in proximity to newspapers, magazines, radio, television, and billboards.

Attempts to shut all those influences out will meet with some success, but then you will be subjected to them secondhand. Recommendations from neighbors, pressure from your peers, and what you see others doing spreads the news equally as well.

Since our world, particularly in capitalistic societies, is completely driven and dependent on sales, national production, and successful profiteering, none of this is going away.

At the beginning of the new millennium, a number of large advertising agencies will begin to purchase their own cable television stations. The reason for this will be apparent by 2005; advertising will become an integral part of the shows that are produced for viewing on these channels.

Seeing our favorite actors/actresses using a specific product within the context of the program will encourage us, ever so subtly, to purchase the product.

As a result, by 2010, there will be a major increase in legal battles between companies over "trademarks." So, now would be a good time to begin registering them, with particular attention to their "gestalt" or overall silhouette, with clarity at a distance, or significant color being important issues.

Internet service providers are already being targeted by major advertising agencies for listing products. This will become a major investment area by 2005.

By 2030, advertising with paper (magazines, newspapers, catalogues, through the mail, etc.) will begin to fade rather rapidly. The primary form of advertising will be through the television screen.

In 2010, the average commercial length will be thirty seconds; by 2020, fifteen seconds; and an all-time low of ten seconds or less by 2050. More of the message will be delivered visually than by sound or through entertaining story lines.

Subscriptions to magazines and newspapers will begin to be handled via encrypted Internet links by 2010, a trend that will not go unnoticed by advertisers. As you sit in front of your computer in the year 2015 reading your favorite article, segmented advertising will be flashing across a strip at the upper and low portions of the screen.

Advertisements will begin to appear in the sky over large cities by night, sometime between 2017 and 2019. Complex, interlaced, multilaser holographic displays will dance off clouds in all the primary colors. At first a great novelty, by 2055 the night sky will be filled with them, much like the neon billboards of today.

Since Global Positioning System equipment will be a standard option for most automobiles by 2012, it will only take a minor modification to use it for advertising. When traveling by auto, you will be able to turn the system on and receive local (within 1000-foot radius) broadcasts from hotels, restaurants, and other facilities, hawking their offerings, prices, and amenities. Today's special is . . . and for only $22.95 . . . only place in town that . . . a hot tub in every room . . . etc. These advertisements will be visual as well as auditory.

Banking

By 2030, there will only be four major banks in America. Their primary competition in most cities will be local credit unions.

Written checks will virtually disappear by 2055. All money transactions will be made by card and electronic thumb- or fingerprint scans at machines.

In 2070, nearly all of the Fortune 2000 corporations will be dealing in home and business mortgaging. Low-income home mortgages will be primarily "government issued." These mortgages will not be person dependent but family dependent. Rather than buying the home outright, families will qualify to live in and maintain them for a percentage of their income. This will make housing affordable for those who are presently unable to buy a home. When the homeowner(s) die, by law they will be able to leave their home to any of their children. If they have no children, then they may leave it to any other blood relative who is willing to maintain it. The mortgage payment will vary, going up or down according to the amount of income received. Because the mortgage payments will be so low, the life of the mortgage will be the life of the home.

A large banking and insurance corporation will attempt to merge in 2008, but will be prevented from doing so by the federal government.

Banking laws will undergo a long string of changes between 2007 and 2025. These issues will primarily have to do with international trade and the specific controls surrounding the movement of large sums of money (between banks)—which will be tightened; the maximum and minimum rate of interest that banks can charge on credit and the method on which it is based; a limitation by law on actions banks can take to recoup losses to individuals—these will not apply to businesses. Accessibility to certain bank records (those records not pertinent to an individual citizen's account) without warrant will be expanded.

By 2040 the responsibility for maintaining an individual's correct credit history will shift to the institutions keeping these records. This will be a result of a number of class-action suits brought between 2028 and 2040.

Individual Retirement Account planning and management will become a big banking business by 2045.

Banks will begin to accept promissory notes for organ donations as collateral for loans after 2030. These will be limited as to which organs.

Financial

According to the current news, a common monetary system will finally be in place within Europe by the year 2000. I predict that it will fluctuate wildly for the first five to seven years. This will have a severe effect on trade with non-European countries. Economies hardest hit as a result will be Mexico, Brazil, Japan, Korea, and China.

We can expect to see a long slide in the stock market (Wall Street) beginning within the next three to six years (probably actually starting around September of 2001.)

There won't be a stock market crash as occurred in the late 1920s, because actions will be taken very swiftly to prevent this from occurring. However, defaults on loans made by, as well as to the United States will increase five to sixfold. Every American can be expected to feel the effects of this in a major way by the year 2003.

As this begins to occur, world productivity will be affected. America is the land of consumers. We buy an enormous amount of goods on an annual basis. As our consumption rate radically falls going into the new millennium, scores of overseas suppliers will begin to feel the cutbacks. Many of the world's economies will suffer as a result. Those who will suffer the most are those who are already feeling the economic crunch.

Inflation will rise significantly in many of the nations we do business with, as well as within our own borders. As a result, interest rates will soar, and the numbers of personal and small business bankruptcies will increase exponentially.

The coming war (see section on war) in the Middle East will add to the problem. Costs will be devastating. By 2010-2012, most Western countries will be suffering economically. Americans won't see relief until perhaps 2075-2080.

The United States will go to a new form of currency by the year 2030. It will vary in size and color, based on denomination. This new currency will predate a North American currency shift by twenty-five years.

Mexico, Canada, and the United States will go to a common currency by 2040. To stabilize the new currency, banks within all three countries will sign agreements of alliance, which will restrict interest and loan rates between countries, and establish certain loan and security agreements.

Before the end of the next century, there will be formal discussions regarding a world currency shift. The new world currency will be based on rates established by a New World Financial Commission, a program initiated by the top ten world financial powers. It will take as long as twenty years to hash out the first steps toward an agreement, and to completely scrub world politics from financial reform. The effect on world trade will be more than significant. Japan and China will play a major part in this reform.

Food Production

There are a number of things that directly affect the production of food: technology, both the kind that's being used to produce the food as well as the kind that addresses the problems that may arise during production—like pests and diseases; the weather; the availability of water; and the ratio of available and appropriate land to end product output—how much land it takes to raise a pig, a cow, or grow a soybean.

At present, we are capable of feeding all the citizens within the United States. There are some countries where this is already not possible. If it were not for the more than heroic efforts of a great deal of people and companies who deal directly with these problems, most of us would already be hungry more days than not.

As an example, most people do not realize that it is only recently (within the past twenty years), that small changes in the genetic structure of rice has enabled a near sixfold increase in world rice production, without requiring ever-increasing amounts of land to be set aside. If these changes in the rice plants had not taken place, a large segment of the world's population would already be dying.

If the chances of hearing a songbird in your yard today are 1 in 10; by the year 2075, they will be reduced to 1 in 1,000, as a direct result of food production methods being utilized.

Within the classification schedule for birds there are thirty-three *orders* (if one counts *suborders*). By the end of the twenty-first century, three complete orders will have vanished, along with at least fourteen *families*, and ninety *species* of birds, all affected by fertilizers and poisons.

By 2040, two species of turtles will have gone the way of the dodo, because of overfishing.

Also as a result of overfishing, some fish will be considered an extreme rarity (if they are not extinct) by the year 2050: the paddle fish, twenty-five species of salmon, trout, char, and whitefish, at least twenty species of cod, six species of tuna, two species of marlin, and two species of sunfish.

While not yet a food source, over two hundred and fifty new species of cockroaches will be discovered in the next fifty years. One will be found to have a tolerance for extreme heat (150°F or more) and a taste for plastics. Consideration of using these insects as a food source for other animals we do eat will become of interest around 2035.

The expansion of the human species will exceed its ability to feed itself by mid-year 2039. This almost seems a ridiculous statement in light of the fact that there are already hungry and starving people in over 90 percent of the world's nations.

There will be dramatic changes in weather that will begin to take place in a significant way between 2022 and 2026. At present, it seems as though the winters are getting milder and the summers a bit hotter. That is exactly what is happening. Summers will begin to get even hotter; as a result they will become even drier, with little or no rain. Winters will become much wetter, with heavy snows. This will have a twofold effect on crops. It will result in the northern spring thaws being delayed further and further south on a year-to-year basis, and the ultra dry summers will result in unexpected erosion of top soil and accelerate the expansion of desert into current crop areas.

By 2028, the average world temperature will have risen two degrees. While this will have in effect moved the second crop-growing season approximately 200 kilometers to the north of where it now resides, further food production won't be possible because the additional heat will reduce the amount of available water by at least 30 percent.

New discoveries in the area of plant genetics between 2019 and 2021 will help boost food production by a sufficient percentage that we do not actually begin to lose ground until 2039.

Water will become a major issue for farmers beginning 2008 to 2014. Existing water sources for food production are already stretched to their limit. Accessing new sources of water will require new rules and regulations regarding water usage for other purposes.

A new strain of rice that thrives on heavier concentrations of saltwater or salt-affected brackish water will be developed by the year 2009. This will increase rice output by as much as 30 percent in the first five years. Other grains will be affected by this same technology within ten years of this date.

By 2021, many large communities will begin to construct wastewater delivery systems to pump the treated city wastewater back onto local farms. The high levels of nitrogen will be good for the crops, but bad for the streams adjacent. Many of the insect, bird, and fish species supported by these natural waterways will be irreparably damaged as a result.

In the year 2050, new methods of sewage processing will be unveiled that not only work more efficiently and better, but from which the by-products become a near 90 percent reusable source of food production materials—providing water, fertilizer, and even power to the cities running these systems.

Six new hybrid fruits will have been discovered by 2015.

Seven hybrid root crops will be genetically manufactured by the year 2020.

Grain production in North America, including Canada, will increase 28 percent by 2045, even with the large reductions in tillable land and the shortage of water resulting from the major weather changes. This will be accomplished by genetically encouraging a stronger grain stalk. With the stronger stalk, it will be able to bear a substantial increase in fruit or seed, perhaps as much as 40 percent.

Because of the demand for larger growing areas, there will be a conscious change by American farmers in their choice of food production. Fewer animals will be grazed on land that can be used for high-yield crops. In 2025, the price of beef will have doubled from its present value per pound. By 2075, beef on any table will be an extreme rarity reserved only for the wealthy.

Fish farms will become a planned-in portion of any farm's operation by the year 2050.

Genetically altered, fast-growing fish from the carp family will be introduced to the family table in 2035. These fish will grow an amazing twelve to sixteen inches, and four to seven pounds per year in relatively small and crowded tanks. They will essentially eat by-products from food-type plant processing—grass clippings and animal manure. Wastewater from these fish-production units will be used on crops as part of an end-of-the-cycle water management program that will begin in the same year.

Those who own a pair of ostriches should hang on to them. This will be the bird of choice for food by 2025. It produces huge amounts of low-cholesterol meat and can be fed those roaches I talked about earlier, along with mush concocted from grain or soybeans, grasshoppers (raised on weeds), and earthworms (raised on sewage mixed with plant by-products). Ostrich feathers can be used for numerous things, and their skin is as tough as any leather.

The single greatest leap in food production will have to do with Euascomycetae and Homobasidiomycetae—morels, truffles, and mushrooms. By 2020, large sections of old mines, government-owned forest floor, and land adjacent to sewage plants will be leased to mushroom growers. In 2035, mushrooms will be advertised as a highly nutritious meat replacement in some meals. Mushrooms are a product that can be cultured and grown on much of the current waste product coming from the production of other foods.

Insurance

By 2050, only one company in America will carry flood insurance—the federal government.

The cost of the average automobile insurance policy will double by the year 2050. One of the ways of reducing automobile insurance will be to sign a waiver refusing insurance against theft. People with "nonvalued" transportation will then get the break.

An insurance company will actually sue one of its own customers between 2010 and 2012 to recoup funds paid out for a drunken-driving fatality.

Term life policies above $25,000 will be twice as hard to qualify for in 2025, three times as difficult by 2050. After 2075, most companies will no longer sell life insurance. It will have been taken over by other investment practices that pay out higher returns.

Manufacturing

All privately owned aircraft within North America will either be experimental or self-constructed by 2075.

Seventy-five percent of all the materials utilized in the manufacture of a house will have to come from recycling by 2050.

A new form of concrete will appear between 2018 and 2020, for use as a roofing material and as an ingredient for walkways. Light to dark gray, it will contain recycled plastics and a significant amount of shredded tires. Nearly indestructible, it will weigh about half as much as current roofing tiles, but last five times longer.

Food irradiation will become the second most popular method for preserving food across the world, by 2050. Many of the foods now requiring freezing or refrigeration (meat, some dairy products, and vegetables), will be sealed in shrink-wrap, irradiated, and be able to withstand temperatures of -30°F to +120°F for periods exceeding one month. This will aid in the distribution of food to Third World countries.

The first automobile constructed entirely from high-impact plastic (except, of course, for the engine and transmission) and for use by the public will be manufactured in 2021.

In 2055 tax breaks will be offered to manufacturing companies based on a rise in their production.

By the middle of the next century, most manufacturing will be accomplished in Africa, South America, and China—least to most, respectively. North America, Europe, and the Far East will be primarily consumers.

There will be manned manufacturing companies established and operating on the surface of the Moon in 2055. Automated manufacturing will be taking place on the surface of Mars and on at least two moons circling another planet by 2075.

A large man-made island will be constructed off the coast of Japan, where manufacturing and industry will be operating above and beneath the sea.

Retailing

In 2070, there will be 75 percent fewer retailers. Direct sales from manufacturers to customers by electronic means will eliminate the need for the retail sales store.

By 2035-2040, most retailers will operate one on one with their customers, consulting directly and personally for sales. Services, as well as things like the selection of clothing, home furnishings, and even food menus, will be handled by retailers who bring them to the customer in a personalized way.

Streamlined manufacturing processes, a severe reduction in resources, and the need to eliminate waste will reduce retail inventories by 90 percent by the year 2040. By 2070, the average customer who needs a pair of shoes will make an appointment with a shoe consultant who will then come to their home and measure their feet. Information regarding the customer's size, desire for design, color preference, and material for the shoes will be forwarded instantly to the manufacturer, who will then produce the shoes and deliver them back to the customer. The entire process will take less than twenty-four hours, and in some cases much less. Payment to the consultant (retailer), the manufacturer, the delivery system, and taxes will all occur automatically and at the same time, at time of purchase.

In 2050, there will be limits on retail sales for some products. A customer's ability to purchase another, or like, item at some future date will be dependent on his or her history of recycling. The retailers who sell the specific item being controlled will maintain a recycling history on customers. Initially, controlled items will be things like cars, boats, appliances, etc., and there will be a differentiation between those items used for home or office. Eventually, these histories will be expanded to include not only items returned for recycling, but lists of items (materials) consumed. The result? By the year 2075, people will be making conscious decisions on where they would like to spend their "wood allowance"—on a new desk or a new bed.

By the dawn of the new century, 2100, people will take pride in their ability to live under Spartan conditions—a small area, minimal furniture, and a single closet for their belongings.

Stock Markets

This is probably the one area for which I have received the most requests for information over the past four or five years. Of course the single biggest questions are "Is it going to crash? When is it going to crash?"

Unlike many who make stock market predictions, I will not equivocate about how I feel about it as a subject. In my opinion, I think it is just one more form of gambling. The market depends on the rise in gross national product as well as the amount of investments being made by people. So there are two truths about the market that will never change:

1. There will always be winners, and there will always be losers.

2. The losers will always outnumber the winners.

In addition, there is a third truth, which everyone should know going in. Stockbrokers will always make money. If the market goes up or down, they make money selling, and they make money buying. Whether you win or lose, they make money. Of course, the amount of money they make is certainly dependent on the numbers of customers they can or can't keep. But, on their worst day, they will make money and a lot of it. They are like the "house" in Vegas.

Having said all that, what happens in the stock market is a direct reflection of the health of the nation. Other countries look at our stock market on a day-to-day basis and make judgments on investing or not investing based on what it is doing. They have their own markets as well. So, there is a certain amount of interaction between markets. When another market suffers a significant fall or enjoys a sudden rise, it eventually affects all the other markets to which it is connected.

Aside from this, there is one more major point you need to know. The markets of the world are not just large amebic and mindless entities that sort of follow the vagaries of economic climate. They are also affected in a great way by some very powerful *individuals* who can, at almost any time, shake them to their core. They can do this by simply raising or lowering the interest rate half a point.

So, if you are looking for guarantees, and you want your savings to be absolutely safe, my recommendation is do not invest in the stock market.

There will be three major historical drops in the American market over the next hundred years. One will begin to occur late in the year 2006. The primary reason for this fall will be a war in the Middle East. This will have a disastrous effect on the European market, which in turn will affect ours.

A second will begin to occur in 2029, following record climatic changes that will affect resources and food production, both having a major negative impact on manufacturing and unemployment. Failures in the Far East market will signal the beginning of this fall.

The third will begin in the year 2056, but I have not been able to ascertain the reasons. I get a sense that there will actually be significant changes in the way the market operates, resulting in this fall to a new point of balance. It could be that the United States market will in some way merge with or be combined with another large market at that time.

There will be other downturns in the market, which are not as significant. These will occur in mid-2000, 2017, 2039, and 2070.

Just as things go down, there are times when things will go up. The two greatest rises in market will be just prior to two of the most significant falls: 2020 and 2050. I've always been a little suspect of these dates for two reasons: they are even dates, and I can't seem to isolate a specific reason for either.

There will be smaller and more long-term rises in the market as well. We are currently in one now, at the expense of our friends in the Far East, and others will occur in 2022, 2031, 2059, and 2088.

Futures on commodities will expand in a big way (more commodities added) between 2005 and 2035. The most significant commodities will be those having to do with materials required in support of alloys necessary to transportation and electronics. Commodities that go into the production of plastics will remain fairly constant through the next fifty years.

The most volatile commodities will be food. Changes in climate will affect this area heavily from now through the year 2070.

The most expansive long-term investment areas will take place in the exploitation of space and space-based resources, like mining and the manufacture of new alloys based on resources mined.

The most expansive Earth-bound investment area will have to do with sea-born construction (the creation of cities, manufacturing facilities, and farms on the water along the coasts.)

Transportation

By the year 2035, the first high-temperature, electromagnetic monorail system will be operating between Los Angeles and Las Vegas. Because of its success, new high-speed monorail systems (trains traveling in excess of 350 miles per hour), will be constructed between Boston and Washington, D.C.; Miami and Atlanta; and St. Louis and Chicago.

By 2075, high-speed monorail systems will also be constructed between Montreal and Toronto; Moscow and Kiev; Moscow and St. Petersburg; Moscow and Rostov; Lisbon and Madrid; Berlin and München, via Frankfurt; and Kuala Lumpur and Singapore.

High-speed trains (not monorails) that travel at speeds exceeding 125 miles per hour will be built in many of the other countries around the world, e.g., connecting the cities of Madras, Bombay, Delhi, and Calcutta, in India; Hanoi to Thanh-Pho Ho Chi Minh City, Vietnam; Bangkok, Thailand, and Viangehan, Laos, etc.

By 2035, nearly all intercontinental flights will be at supersonic speeds. However, these planes will not produce shock waves. New technology will permit flight at speeds in excess of mach three, with very little air disturbance.

In 2075, NASA will have an operational ground-to-space plane, which will operate from runways, travel into space, and return. This will allow for space flight access to civilians.

These planes will service satellites in low orbit, as well as supply and maintain the new Multinational Space Platform.

Please note that I believe this plane already exists, but is currently classified. In its current configuration (see drawing below), there are problems with shock-wave interactions on reentry, as well as with the current experimental engine design.

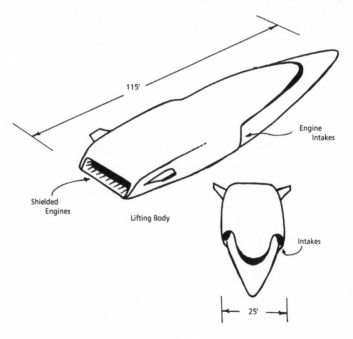

The engine currently has a "morphing" capability, by which it changes its appearance and operation radically while in flight. These issues will be ironed out by 2020, and the plane will be declassified by 2025. The reason for its eventual declassification will be a radical new concept in propulsion that will not be shared with civilians until the early 2050s.

By the year 2050, travel between cities will employ a new form of fan-jet, which will halve the current fuel consumption and produce less than one-fourth the pollution of a standard intercity jet or turboprop of today.

Takeoff and landing requirements will be reduced by over half, resulting from a type of "morphing" (deforming and reforming) wing design while in flight. Inherent in these designs will be the elimination of icing as an in-flight problem during winter operation.

These radical new designs will also reduce the rough ride characteristics associated with air anomalies—in particular wind shear.

By 2010, two manufacturers will unveil a new type of helicopter that will operate as a vertical takeoff and landing vehicle that will operate as a fixed-wing aircraft. Unlike the current models that operate by rotating the lifting props from a horizontal to a vertical position, this particular aircraft will shift its lifting drive to a horizontal drive mechanism, freezing the lifting props into a fixed or lifting wing configuration (see drawings next page).

Sometime around the year 2026, auto manufacturers will unveil two new types of engines. Both will operate based on a kinetic energy storage system using a type of flywheel, married to a hybrid engine. One will be powered by hydrogen, which it will actually separate from an on-board water supply, and one will be electrically powered and based on a new form of long-term electrical storage system, having to do with an exotic metallic/chemical alloy or mix.

With the completion of its new dam, China will begin investing huge sums in the development of intercity transportation by electric passenger car sometime after 2025.

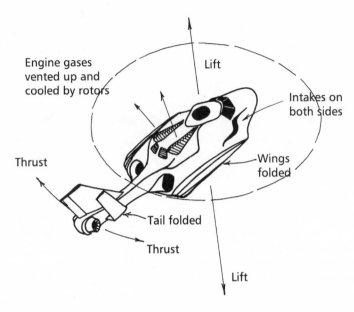

Engine gases vented up and cooled by rotors

Lift

Intakes on both sides

Thrust

Wings folded

Tail folded

Thrust

Lift

By 2025, there will be at least four cities in America that forbid the use of vehicles other than bicycles inside their city limits (with the exception of vehicles used for delivery of materials and supplies, of course). By 2060, this will have spread to over a third of the cities in America with populations exceeding 4 million.

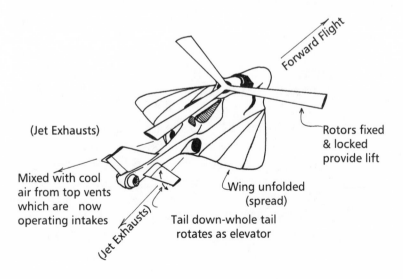

Forward Flight

(Jet Exhausts)

Rotors fixed & locked provide lift

Mixed with cool air from top vents which are now operating intakes

Wing unfolded (spread)

(Jet Exhausts)

Tail down-whole tail rotates as elevator

What will make this work will be the establishment of rings of car parks just inside the first half of the city proper, which are interconnected by electric trains and/or bus systems.

Computer-managed vehicles will be encouraged by 2030; by 2075, no vehicle will be manually operated except as a condition of emergency.

Before 2005, a business group will either purchase a large Russian submarine, or have one built. The purpose will be for the transport of materials and goods. In the place of missile tubes, it will carry pressurized containers of cargo.

Later versions of this sub will have large container systems that will actually connect or buckle directly to the sides of the sub.

The reasons for building such container vessels will be to preclude delays caused by weather and to make faster cross-ocean trips possible. These cargo-carrying submarines will have the capacity of maintaining speeds that average forty knots in all kinds of weather. They will also be nuclear powered.

A solid object four inches in diameter will actually be teletransported from a point A to a point B, by the year 2050. The power requirement to do this transport will preclude using the system for larger objects until the beginning of the next century. Live objects will not be transported for some time after that.

13

ENVIRONMENT

Air

Air quality will continue to degrade well into the next century. By 2050, many businesses will be doing more to the air their employees are breathing inside their buildings than cooling or heating it. After 2025, new forms of air scrubbers will be designed to remove toxins, carbon dioxide, and other elements that are building up in the atmospheres of our homes, workspaces, and areas in which we congregate.

By then, allergies will be so severe in children, it will be considered a national epidemic.

Initially, air scrubbing will only be affordable in areas where large groups congregate: workspaces, shopping centers, movie theaters, meeting halls, restaurants, hotels, and the like. But by mid-century, they will be utilized in at least a fourth of the privately owned homes in America.

By 2040, disposal of the air scrubber filters will become a major problem, almost equaling nuclear waste. In fact, in some areas, the air filters will be stored with or eliminated in conjunction with nuclear waste.

A major effort at "greening" the planet will begin around 2015. Initially it will have very little effect, but eventually (2080-2090) it will have caught up to and repaired much of the damage done in this next century. The greening effort will begin in China with a single week of planting trees. This event will be the largest of its kind in the history of mankind.

Over a single week, the Chinese people will plant over 125 billion small saplings, or what will become known as the "trees of life." This effort will be followed by like efforts in Russia, Southeast Asia, South America, North America, India, Africa, and the Middle East. In a two-year period, the human race will replace all the trees cut over a two-hundred-year period. More than half will be properly cared for and survive.

Aerosols considered harmful to air quality will be slowly eliminated from products between now and the year 2060. The greatest difficulty in this elimination will come from North Americans.

A way of using an electromagnetic-magnetic wave-front to clarify air will be discovered by 2022. It will be formally tested on upper-atmosphere air regions by the year 2051. Much controversy will surround this methodology, as it will also prove harmful to migratory birds.

The air quality index will have a major impact on whether or not we venture from our houses by the year 2033.

Biology

In 2025, there will be a concerted effort to genetically alter/manufacture new species of birds—specifically songbirds.

By the year 2030, techniques will exist for the creation of "designer animals." Originally developed for the pet industry, there will be toy goats, toy deer, toy (half the size of miniature) horses, palm-sized raccoons, etc.

Farmers will realize the technology's value for producing more for less, and leaner meat, per acre. In 2010, flightless chickens weighing more than thirty pounds will appear on the market.

By 2050 new, designer-type meats like a super snake, a cross between a camel and a horse, and something akin to a fur-covered pig will appear.

By 2015, scientists will develop a new form of bacterium through gene splicing. This bacterium will be able to consume large amounts of petrochemical toxins and agents at waste disposal sites, converting them into an effluent solution that can be electromagnetically separated and filtered from the containment medium at a very cheap rate.

When we reach the year 2075, mankind will have lost so many biological species that the continued existence of biodiversity itself will be threatened. Legal action will be taken to protect what remaining biological species there are from any further damage as a result of individual action. Species deliberately harmed by individuals will result in stiff punishments and heavy fines. This will carry over into the world court.

Genetic reproductive problems in mankind will reach a significant level by 2035. The eventual destruction of our own species will become a major topic as a result. Because the Human Genome Project will have been completed by then, efforts to develop methods for reintroducing important gene structures into our offspring will be undertaken. In other words, we will be able to shop for intelligence, physical strength, height, or good eyesight by the year 2050.

This genetic manipulation will not be without its problems. Sometime between 2022 and 2028, a researcher will be tried in a court of law for producing a surviving human nightmare in *her* lab, using her own body as the breeding ground.

Bridges

Early in the new century, between 2008 and 2010, a decision will be made to replace over half of the nonsuspension bridges in America. Over half of those will be replaced with single-strand suspension bridges.

A section of the Verrazano-Narrows Bridge, in New York City, will collapse sometime between 2012 and 2016.

Following a disastrous fire above the twenty-fifth floor of a New York high-rise building in 2022, a decision will be made to interconnect all buildings above fourteen floors whenever possible, with an enclosed walkway. Originally intended as an emergency fire escape to an adjacent building, people will begin to use them for day-to-day living and refer to them as skybridges.

The last remaining wood-covered bridge will cease to exist in extreme north-central Vermont sometime between the years 2021 and 2023.

The interconnecting bridges between the various keys south of Miami will be abandoned between 2038 and 2040, due to rising tides.

Cities

Cities are already going underground. Interconnected walkways, stores, restaurants, etc., are ideally maintained in the underground environment, especially where climatic conditions require it. By the middle of the next century, almost all cities with a population exceeding 1 million people will have centralized underground complexes with controlled climate conditions.

The single greatest threat to modern cities along the coast is the continuing rise in average tides. By 2025, high tide will breach the current sea wall heights along most of the northeast United States. Cities located along the edges of the Great Lakes, as well as the Gulf and West Coasts of the United States are also at risk. By 2050, sections of Boston; New York; New Jersey; Philadelphia; Washington, D.C.; Miami; New Orleans; Houston; Los Angeles; San Francisco; and Seattle will be abandoned. Buildings subjected to saltwater soaking will self-destruct through decay in less than ten years' time.

The city of Key West will be all but abandoned by the year 2045.

Cities along the coastlines of Europe and the Far East will suffer the same fate within the same time window. Attempts to build dikes to prevent the rise in water levels will generally meet with disaster.

The first and largest underground city in the world will be constructed in Western Australia along the coast north of Perth by 2035. The desert building techniques polished and perfected in Australia will be exported to the Middle East and North Africa beginning around 2019.

Cities built on platforms will begin to appear very early in the next century. The first will be completed in Japan by the year 2030. Well, actually it will never be completed, because they will work on it continuously once it is started. It will be a city constructed on a platform that floats on water but that cannot be moved. Only the very wealthy will live on this platform, as the day-to-day fees for maintaining this first effort will be extremely high.

Miniature floating cities will be constructed in the form of ships, beginning around 2015. The first of these will actually be launched in 2025 amidst great fanfare. About the size of two aircraft carriers lashed side to side, it will be twin-hulled, with no less than sixty watertight compartments. Powered by nuclear engines, this monster ship will be capable of moving from port to port. Its greatest attractiveness will be the number of oceanfront condos and the fact that it can move from north to south or vice versa, for winter or summer living. Maintenance and service support personnel will live in the bowels of these floating cities, which will number nine by the end of the century. These endeavors will require new forms of international treaties and oceangoing passports will evolve as a result.

Buildings

More and more recyclable materials will be going into both new and old buildings by 2010. Nearly all new construction will use frameworks of recycled metals and plastics. By 2020, about 45 percent of new construction will contain recycled materials—by 2050, over 90 percent.

Common features in the houses of 2025 will include the following:

1. Windows that not only go from fogged to clear with the touch of a dial, but also change colors, and are capable of producing a background picture; e.g., sunny day with a garden, night view of a large cityscape, etc.

2. Rudimentary garbage and sewage processing and recycling; e.g., brownwater production capability, rainwater collection and purification capability, natural heat collection and storage, and supplemental electrical energy collection. Extra energy collected but not used will be automatically fed back into the energy delivery system (power grid).

3. Shared, or common, walls with another home; e.g., duplex, triplex, or quadriplex living.

4. High-impact, easy-to-clean, interior walls made from recycled materials that have built-in finishes; e.g. rough, pebbly, sandy, woven, etc. Recycled materials will be molded one into the other, eliminating many of the now well-defined 90-degree joints found on most walls at corners, replacing them with smooth, multidegree curves instead.

5. All lighting will be low voltage and use long-duration bulbs.

6. Wood flooring and wall-to-wall carpeting will be two of the most expensive options in the house of tomorrow.

7. Foundations will be monolithic pours of a new material that will combine cements with recycled materials, to include reprocessed automobile tires. They will

provide for a 40 percent increase in insulation value, extreme protection against water seepage, and virtually eliminate ground pollutant problems.

8. Interior or exterior use of wood will begin to disappear, except for specific trim purposes, about this time.

By the year 2075:

1. Housing will all be multi-unit; single-family dwellings will be terribly expensive to own and operate.

2. Nearly 100 percent of the home will be constructed from recycled materials.

3. The average square footage will have been reduced to approximately 1,100 square feet for a family of four in America—probably 900 square feet in Europe.

4. Houses will be 100 percent electronically controlled by voice, as well as by sensing the needs of the family's bodies. Furniture, heat, light, and ambient music will be automatically modified for preset conditions fitting the specific person who is using them, or the room, at the time.

5. False windows and doors will present images of the outdoors, and create an impression of a single-family dwelling for most condos and apartments.

6. You will be able to communicate with your home from a distance, and the home electronic system will arrange for necessary cleaning, or preparations required for entertaining guests. As an example, the cleaning person will have a prearranged security pass

that the house recognizes and the house will make all arrangements for cleaning itself, without your required participation.

7. All homes will have a "Virtual Room," where one can go to seek entertainment, visit almost any place in the world, or participate in a personal game selection. So, one could arrange to enter the room on Fridays, as an example, for a weekly poker night, where you might interact with a group of virtual or holographic players.

For most people who are occupied in information-oriented types of jobs, the home and workspace will be the same by the year 2025. Companies will exist completely within cyberspace. You'll be able to visit with your employees or observe what they are doing at any time electronically.

People with severe medical problems will have their bodies electronically wired into the local 911 systems. The house will monitor their physical condition and automatically notify emergency personnel when it senses distress that may lead to a severe medical problem. This will be in place by 2040.

Also, by 2045, most people will make trips to their doctors for routine checkups via cyberspace. Sitting in the control chair and inserting one's arm into a "reader" will be all that is required for doctors to do this normal checkup. (See under medical technology for more.)

Forests

We will begin to eliminate most of the now-existing roads into our national forests by the year 2018. This will be an attempt at bringing them back to their natural ecological state.

We will begin to section off our national forests with ½- to ¾-mile-wide strips or fire breaks in 2025. The idea is that when fires begin as a result of natural causes (lightning), we will let nature take its course—and let them burn.

The hunting laws in America will be nationalized by 2020. This will result from a need to control the populations of certain animals within national forests. This will also be a result of a rash of overreactions to bear attacks, which will take place along the eastern Blue Ridge Mountains between 2017 and 2019. Gun control will have a strong bearing on these issues as well as on enforcement, cross-state hunting, and licensing.

There will be a 30 percent increase in protected wetlands as a result of the rise in average tides by 2030.

By 2030, only half the current number of lumber mills will survive; by 2050, only a third. Aside from "manufactured" timbers, expect raw lumber to be excessively expensive by the beginning of the second half of the next century. An exposed beam within a house will be looked on with disdain instead of in a positive way—much as people currently view fur coats.

By 2075, visiting a forest will be the same as visiting a zoo. We will slowly begin to eliminate man-controlled zoos by 2060. The only zoos existing in 2100 will be breeder farms run by researchers. They will not be open to the public.

The American chestnut tree will once again be growing strong in most areas of America's deciduous forests by 2070. The sugar maple, most species of elms, and longleaf pine will be near extinction.

Large sections (20 percent) of deciduous forests in the northeast will be taken over by pines before 2060. As if on cue, hardwoods will begin springing up below snow lines across many of the evergreen forests of the Southwest and Northwest by the end of the next century.

In 2050, the greatest importer of wood in the world will be China. Second greatest will be Germany. As an added note, the Black Forest of Germany will cease to exist by the year 2075. The primary cause will be a need for space, followed by the poor condition of the forest itself.

In the second decade of the new millennium, a new international organization will come into existence, with the sole purpose of managing the remaining world's rain forests. They will accomplish this by setting up and controlling funds for the payment of lease fees to the governments who control the rain forest territories.

These management responsibilities will include the setting of strict rules, requirements, and fees for other interests taking place within the rain forests, such as the removal of minerals, erosion from adjacent farming, or access by pharmaceutical research companies, etc.

Geology

New diamond mines will be discovered in South America by 2020. There will also be a diamond discovery in central Australia by the year 2025.

The largest and oldest gemstone mines in the world will be discovered just east of the Ural Mountains in Russia beginning in 2014. Within ten years of discovery, they will produce the world's largest garnet, emerald, and pigeon blood ruby ever cut and polished.

The largest yellow diamond in history will be discovered in the mountains of Arkansas, between 2031 and 2035.

A new string of islands will begin to form in the middle of the Pacific Ocean halfway between the islands of Japan and Hawaii. The first will break the surface around 2041, following a huge underwater eruption that will essentially go on for a period of nine years.

Following the discovery of heavy metals, and copper, between 2016 and 2018, six nations will agree to begin exploring Antarctica for the purposes of mining by 2020. This will lead to a territorial treaty that cuts Antarctica up into small states, one of which will be United Nations controlled.

China will begin to reclaim desert in the next century, through the development of hybrid grasses that can be fed with seawater pumped from the ocean (around 2023). This slow but successful reclamation program will be the model followed by most of the Middle Eastern nations which will begin their own efforts in earnest by 2030. All these innovative practices will have been developed and shared with the East by the scientists of Israel.

Highways

Fully automated, or computer controlled highways, will be tested by 2005. The first of these highways will be introduced for use in 2010. It will be a road somewhere in the Southwest, probably in the state of Texas, or New Mexico. Most roads in America as well as Europe will be fully automated or run by computers by the year 2050.

What I am referring to here are roads that automatically interact with the automobile. The driver will essentially give over control of the vehicle to the road itself, which will modulate speed, lane, and egress at a preselected or chosen point. The driver will be required to simply monitor the activities of the automobile.

A new surfacing material will be introduced to highways by 2015. It will be made from a 50/50 mixture of new and recycled materials. This new surface will wear considerably longer than any in existence today, and be able to withstand weathering much better than current roads.

One of the reasons this surface will wear better will be the invention of a new rubber/metal alloy, from which tires will be constructed beginning in 2010. These new tires will grip the road better, operate 30 percent more efficiently on wet surfaces, and require no air. The air will be integral to its constructed form, sort of like bubbles in egg whites.

Nearly all trans-state roads, that is roads crisscrossing states will be four lanes by 2050. There will only be ingress/egress points approximately every five to eight miles.

Secondary or parallel roads will be constructed along their sides for local access.

Speed limits on all state roads will be 80 MPH by 2025. Speed limits on side or parallel service roads will never exceed 40 MPH.

Highway emergency notifications, advertisements for gas, lodging, restaurants, or updates on traffic will be automatically relayed to the car radio from a subsurface wire along both sides of the road by 2028. Information will differ depending on the direction in which you are traveling.

General directions and maps will all be electronic and displayed on a heads-up windscreen display beginning in 2015. These displays will be delivered by satellite automatically for a small service fee, and coordinated by Global Positioning Systems overhead. Emergencies will be automatically reported to local service stations by the automobile, and these will be monitored by the highway patrol.

By 2020, most vehicles will also be able to respond to identity checks by police. They won't give out personal information, like name or occupants, but they will say whether or not they are operating under a privately registered (maybe AAA) drive plan (DP). In the case of a specific criminal event within an area, warrants could be obtained at a later date to study site- and time-specific DPs. Lack of a registered DP would automatically notify police of the vehicle's immediate location and direction of travel.

DPs, as described above, will be used for tracking inter-state commerce by truck before 2020. Based on the information obtained, licensing and trucking usage fees will be reduced for those who do not do as much hauling, and increased for those who do.

Large trucking companies will be using this system of tracking before it is generally accepted by the public.

By 2030, the federal government will require states to provide a one-mile section of highway every thirty miles that can be used as an emergency runway for aircraft. This means the section of road will have to be nearly flat, straight, and have collapsible center divider stanchions. It will also be marked with solar- and battery-powered low-wattage lamps.

Nearly all cities above 20,000 population will have cameras mounted on lights at intersections by 2020. These will be used to monitor traffic, and photograph both speeders as well as red/caution light runners. Most of these cameras will have a remote control capability for scanning adjacent sidewalks and business storefronts as well, and will be undetectable as an integral part of the streetlight.

All multipassenger speed lanes, regulated for rush hour traffic, will be computer controlled by 2025.

Land

The single greatest return on investment in 2050 will be land. Buy dirt now!

By the year 2025, farming land will be reduced by 20 percent.

Wetlands will increase substantially by 2050, mainly due to the rise in tides.

By 2025, the states with

1. The greatest land problems will be Arizona and Florida.

2. The greatest amounts of available land will be Idaho, North Dakota, South Dakota, and Washington State.

3. The greatest number of lost persons will be in New York, especially in the upstate area and the Catskill and upper Adirondack Mountains. It will hold that honor because of its naturally rugged and inaccessible

terrain, which prevents normal search-and-rescue operations being used in other states.

4. The most expensive land in America will be Connecticut, California, and Oregon.

5. The cheapest land in America will be Texas and Montana.

There will be a great push to reopen to private sale land currently held by the federal government. This will result in the Great Land Act being passed around 2029. About half the land will be sold in twenty-five-acre plots to nonbusiness citizens, the other half will go to a land trust, which can be commonly utilized through a new form of licensing.

Marine

Privately owned and operated submarines will be in vogue by 2010. These will be diesel powered, but capable of ninety-day journeys. They will be operated like private motor yachts.

The first fully automatic, nonmanned, atomic-powered, self-contained robotics research submarine will be launched around 2025. Its job will be to cruise the bottom of the sea in search of minerals. It will surface only once a month, when it will burst-transmit its location and findings, and receive its new instructions from its mother ship via satellite.

Eight new sources of food products will be discovered through marine biology by 2020. However, the real accomplishment will be the discovery of sixteen new medicines before 2040. Most of these new medicines will be useful in the treatment of bone diseases, neurological disorders, and cancer.

Permanent underwater fish farms will be constructed by 2030, and will be manned in one-month shifts. Fish will be grown, harvested, and shipped via submersible tube to the surface cleaning facilities, much like oil is now pumped from ships offshore through long underwater pipes.

By 2025, a new kind of oil platform will be designed that can be operated while totally submerged. These will be towed into place by boat, and serviced with utility submarines. By anchoring these to the seabed, they will not be exposed to surface weather. They will, therefore, be much smaller and cheaper to operate.

Fishing rights will become a very major issue in the first third of the twenty-first century. There will be symposiums hosted by the United Nations before 2010, to discuss the possible partitioning of the oceans for marine resources. These meetings will initially be called to address fishing rights beyond what are now considered coastal limits along national boundaries. Resources will be addressed as a separate issue from requirements for transportation, policing, or defense. Concerns will center on those countries that have no natural access to the sea. These problems will initially be addressed by the issuing of dividends for certain import materials—like fish, magnesium, or other ores. This will only be a temporary fix, however, as these issues will continue throughout the next hundred years.

The hunting of whales will continue till approximately 2015, when at least two species will be declared extinct. A world moratorium will be put into effect, which will last until 2050. There will be violations of this moratorium in the first fifteen years, during which "resource pirates" will be caught and tried for these offenses. Eventually, by the year 2050, whales will no longer be hunted on the high seas.

Half the current species of sharks will be near extinction by the year 2030. No one will care. The balance of those remaining will be hunted well into the '70s. Eventually, the hunting will cease and some species of shark will regenerate, only because there are so few fishing for them by then.

Because natural reefs will continue to degrade, mankind will make a concerted effort to increase the creation or building of new offshore reefs. This will be done primarily through the sinking of boats and barges, and the dumping of concrete and other debris that is essentially fish and water friendly.

By 2033, scientists will have learned to breed and raise some of the great game fish, adding a great deal back into the natural stocks.

General marine ordinances will be adopted by the United Nations between 2019 and 2025. These will be enforced by the navies of the UN membership. Violators will have their ships confiscated and will be tried in world court.

Natural Disasters

When you open the book to natural disasters, you are opening one of the greatest areas of human fear. I don't know why that is true, but it seems to be so. Over the years I have probably gotten more questions about pending natural disasters than any other area or topic. People are worried about how their money, homes, lives, or jobs might be directly affected by what happens naturally.

First, let me say that no one on the face of the planet is immune from natural disasters. Those who live where earthquakes are rare may be prone to flooding. Those who never see any flooding can be devastated by tornadoes overnight, and so on and so forth.

The place in which I live, Nelson County, Virginia, lies within the foothills of the Blue Ridge Mountains and is one of the least threatening places you can imagine. However, in 1969, over a hundred and fifty people were killed by Hurricane Camille, which crossed half the continent to dump twenty-seven inches of rain in eight hours here. The flash floods that this rain started were horrible. Whole sections of roadway, steel and concrete bridges, and the sides of mountains were literally swept away. Some people's cars, trucks, and houses disappeared into the night and were literally never seen again. Who would have suspected? Miami maybe, or the Florida Keys, but never the foothills of Virginia.

Well, Mother Nature doesn't work that way. As a living and breathing entity, our Earth is expected to grow, change, and sometimes become violent. Earth has a right. We as fleas on the Earth's back will usually suffer the consequences.

I generally don't like making predictions about natural disasters for the following reasons:

1. Such predictions sometimes create severe anxiety in people who then go off and do drastic things as a result, like selling their homes or quitting their jobs and moving.

2. While many times the predictions will be true, many times they aren't. Time is very difficult to pin down when it comes to Mother Nature, as any geologist or vulcanologist will tell you.

3. There is too much focus on the negative, or on something we can do very little about.

Having said all this, I must now talk about natural disasters, or most of my friends won't buy this book. I'll begin with earthquakes.

I can tell you with near certainty that there will be significant earthquakes over the next one hundred years in southern Alaska; the San Francisco, Los Angeles, and San Diego areas of California; Mexico City; Guatemala; Northern Peru, Bolivia; and southern Chile on the American continent. Other sites will include North Africa, Sicily, the Black and Caspian Sea areas, Iran, Pakistan, India, South and Central China, the Philippines, and Japan. What do I mean by "significant"? They will register at least 8.5 to 8.8 on the Richter scale. They will be killer quakes.

Attaching years to them, I can say that in all probability they will occur within five years, plus or minus, of the following dates:

Year	Place
2013	Qom, Iran
2013-2015	Los Angeles, California
2018	Near Catania, Sicily
2022	Near Sivas, Turkey, south of the Black Sea
2022-2023	San Francisco, California
2026	Near Makhachkala, on the Caspian Sea
2028	Near Multan, in Central Pakistan
2031	Mexico City, Mexico
2033	Near Lanzhou, in Central China
2038	175 miles east of Guatemala
2039	Between Nagoya and Matsusaka, Japan
2041	Just inland from Valdivia, in southern Chile
2044	Between Trujillo and Chiclaao, in northern Peru
2050	Upstate New York
2056	100 miles south of La Paz, Bolivia
2056	Near Amravati, in Central India
2056	Central Mindanao, Philippines
2061	San Diego, California
2071	Near Beskra, Algeria, in Northern Africa

Year	Place
2077	Between Anchorage and Kenai, Alaska
2078	Near Hengyang, in South China

Of all these quakes, the one occurring in Upstate New York will probably be the most devastating for Americans. It will be the most expensive natural disaster in the history of our country.

The most serious quake in other regions of the world will occur just outside of Lanzhou, in central China. It will cause the greatest loss of life.

There will be a major volcanic eruption in Washington State sometime between 2026 and 2030. While not as large as Mount St. Helens, it will cause more damage and loss of life. There will be significant volcanic action in the Hawaiian Islands between 2014 and 2023, resulting in the abandonment of a now-occupied island. Popocatépetl, just south of Mexico City, will erupt between 2029 and 2031. There will be significant damage from the initial blast, but not as great a loss of life as might be expected from being so close to such a large city.

And, of course, I have already talked about the birth of a new chain of islands in the Pacific Ocean between Japan and Hawaii in an earlier section.

Aside from the above, the following are also major eruption areas that will cook off in the next hundred years.

Dates	Places
Between now and 2005	Kamchatka, Russia
Between now and 2005	Indonesia
Between 2008 and 2014	Soufriere, St. Vincent
Between 2010 and 2015	Surtsey, Iceland

Dates	Places
Between 2011 and 2016	Northwestern Iran
Between 2019 and 2023	Near Kilimanjaro, Africa
Between 2020 and 2025	Taal, Luzon, Philippines
Between 2021 and 2024	Quizapu, Chile
Between 2045 and 2050	El Chichon, Mexico
Between 2050 and 2055	Santa Maria, Guatemala
Between 2066 and 2073	Papua, New Guinea

By 2035, fresh water will be a major issue within the United States, specifically in Florida, Colorado, Arizona, California, New Mexico, Nevada, and throughout most of Texas. Interstate water agreements will be worked out for sharing. The primary impact will be on movement of citizens. No new building will be allowed in areas of these states post 2040.

By 2030, flooding will become a much more frequent occurrence within the lowland areas of North America, especially along the major rivers in the Midwest.

By the year 2041, some sections of major world cities will be abandoned or converted to uses other than residential and business, as a result of the changes in climate and the constant rises in water levels. Sections of some cities will be leveled to create the foundation for replacement cities, which will then be built up over them—on higher ground.

By the end of 2050, we will begin to see a substantial rise in the average water level along the coasts of the world. By that time, drinkable water will become a major issue.

By the year 2038, we will begin to see a rise in the average sea level. The average rise in water level will be 2.5 to 4 feet. This will be due to a radical melting of the Arctic and Antarctic polar icecaps. The melting has already started, but as we progress to 2038, this process will begin to accelerate. Most of the northern and southern icecaps will be gone from the face of the Earth by 2080.

The results of the constant rise in water level will cost the American taxpayer over six trillion dollars in damage to existing buildings and infrastructure along current shorelines by the year 2050. Most of this damage will be the result of increasingly severe storms—a secondary problem stemming from the changes in climate as a result of the meltdown.

In 2044, northern states will be called upon to create watershed regions for supplying those states with minimal drinking water supplies. By 2055, the North and South American continents will be crisscrossed with a significant number of fresh water supply pipelines, all running north and south.

Also as a result of weather changes, hurricanes will become much more frequent and much more deadly. By 2025, the United States will be averaging twenty-five to thirty hurricanes a year. At least two of these will be killer storms. People will begin to abandon island living in the Bahamas and the Virgin Islands.

The states that will be most severely affected by these hurricanes are Texas, Alabama, and North Carolina, where beach erosion and tidal surges will destroy extensive areas of property. Florida will suffer, but because of the way it has been constructed, it will weather these storms the best.

Planetary Issues

This is a section of my predictions for which I've always seemed to get mixed support. There are a number of people with whom I've discussed these topics who feel that by addressing such issues I may, in some way, be damaging the credibility of my book. There are, of course, others who feel these things should be included in the book at any cost, because they are important issues.

I've chosen to include them because of recent articles in the *Washington Post*, specifically a headline in the Sunday edition, April 12, 1998, that read

"Crying wolf over asteroids leads to new guidelines."

The subtitling read "NASA officials drew up guidelines to prevent a repeat of what they consider an embarrassing false alarm that threatened Earth with an asteroid collision a month ago."

The rest of the article goes on to talk about NASA's responsibility to the American public and how they are now contemplating additional guidelines that will prevent this from occurring again. They want such future news reported only to specific departments within NASA, where groups of NASA professionals can then go over the materials and, after due consideration, decide the veracity of the material and decide what should or shouldn't be reported publicly.

I translate this to mean *censorship!* It is totally unacceptable. If we let a handful of people decide what "we the public can handle or not handle," we are entering very dangerous waters indeed. I especially resent it when it comes from an agency that deals with matters that are and should be open, and do not concern or relate to national security. We pay your salary, NASA! Every ship you launch, every study you make, and every photograph you take belongs to the American public. In a greater sense, simply because we can afford it and others can't, it probably belongs to the rest of the planet and all of humanity as well.

Having said this, it would be remiss of me not to include something that I have also collected. Hence my decision to include the material in this section. I will trust in the public to temper what I say with caution, and respect it for what it is—simply psychic information, unproven, unverified, and possibly wrong.

Sometime in the year 2016, an asteroid will bypass Earth, missing our globe by less than 1.3 million miles. It will be large enough to cause a measurable electromagnetic effect on the Earth's surface. This will be the first of four that will visit our neighborhood over the next hundred years. The second will pass around 2030, the third in 2044, and the fourth in 2071. None of these rocks will strike our planet.

However, we can expect a large impact from an asteroid exceeding 1.5 kilometers in size by the year 2200. This event will probably occur closer to our next century than toward the end of the second—or sometime between 2120 and 2130.

While there should be some concern, there should be no reason for panic. The events surrounding such an impact as presented by the media are not accurate. While damage will be extensive within a thousand-mile radius of the landing site, it will not create a firestorm that will burn up the Earth's atmosphere, or shift the planet on its axis. It will shake hell out of things and there is a slim possibility that humankind's diet will change drastically overnight, but the species will survive.

The other reason we will survive is because by that time, we will have the capacity for steering, delaying, or altering much of the asteroid's course, if not breaking it up completely.

By the year 2010, astrophysicists will discover at least four or five other M-Class stars in our galaxy. We will verify that all of them possess planets within five years of their discovery.

Planet X, the tenth planet in our solar system, will be verified in the year 2015. It will have an elliptical orbit with a mean distance from the Sun of 51.50 AU, and a density approximately equal to that of Mercury. The discovery will be a result of modifications to an Earth-bound telescope of more than twelve meters, which has not yet been completed (constructed).

Believe it or not, there are "Unidentified Flying Objects (UFOs)." The problem is that we think of this phenomenon in this way, and are probably too quick to associate them with the existence of extraterrestrial beings.

Truth is, there are probably extraterrestrial beings as well, but the two do not necessarily go together. In other words, one does not necessarily lead to the other.

I believe that by the year 2020, sufficient hard proof will exist to establish that UFOs are real vehicles, and are probably piloted by intelligent beings. But, it will take another forty years to establish where they come from.

Sometime after mid-century, we will establish that these vehicles are probably, for lack of a better word, time machines. The question of whether they come from our future or our past will be moot, since we will discover about the same time that time as a construct, does not operate as we have assumed it does until that point.

By 2075, we will have a working understanding of how we can violate time in the same way we have violated space—by simply moving through it. Movement in time will also establish that reality is not just linear, in either space or time modalities, but actually consists of an array of universal constructs that we have, until that point, ignored. Near-instantaneous travel over great distances will also become moot, since the perceived laws surrounding the prohibition of such travel will fade by the end of the next century.

While this prediction makes it all sound real easy, it won't be. The effects these discoveries will have on the self-designated guardians of our spiritual precepts will be profound. It will make for a tough and uphill fight, to keep the topic within a realm of responsible science and religious evaluation, and not let it fall prey to aberrant interpretation, twisted remystification, or a medieval-style persecution.

Also as a result, formal contact with other intelligent beings will take place sometime between 2075 and 2077. This contact will be at their instigation, not ours. We will discover that they are from another *time and space*, just because they have traveled to us. They will bring nothing, nor give us anything that will help us, except the knowledge that we are not alone and that we are on the right track.

By 2025, the nations of the Earth will be operating from an expanding space station, high in orbit around the Earth. Off to a rough start, with a launch just after the change to a new millennium, this space station will accelerate as a result of new discoveries in space flight, e.g., development of a space plane that can take off and land from runways with large payloads.

By the year 2050, civilians will be visiting a second space station that will be privately owned and financed by a consortium of six large corporations. For the small price of two million dollars, you will be able to spend a week in space, drinking vodka martinis.

Construction of an Earth/Moon Bus will begin before 2025; by 2070, we will have an operational base on the Moon, where new methods of manufacturing will be established for primarily producing exotic drugs and metal alloys for electronics. These are the beginnings of the electronic systems that will usher in our understanding of space/time travel, as well as produce unlimited supplies of power.

Attempts to utilize robotic vehicles to collect and carry ore-bearing asteroids into Earth orbit will be made just prior to the turn of the century (2100).

Information collection satellites will circle most of our sister planets by 2050, and we will discover at least two of those planets have basic forms of life extant on their surfaces—Venus and Saturn.

By 2035, we will confirm that life existed at one time on Mars, but probably did not develop there. Life arrived there on a crashed vehicle from another time/space, and certainly from a much earlier age than our own.

A coherent signal will be discovered emanating from another planet, in another solar system within our galaxy by 2018. While the signal will make no sense to us, it will aid in our discovery that we are not alone.

Weather

We will know how to create clouds and produce rain in selected places of the Earth's surface by the year 2015. This will virtually eliminate drought in narrow or selected areas. However, changing the weather in one location will significantly alter the weather in others. These issues will become of interest to the world court by 2025.

On the other hand, Western Europe will suffer a significant drought between 2018 and 2024. This will be a direct result of 2.5- to 3.5-degree water temperature changes in the North Atlantic, due to polar ice melt.

By the year 2026, scientists will successfully demonstrate the ability to make significant changes in weather patterns across the American Midwest. These interruptions in normal weather patterns will create a conflict between the United States, Canada, and Western Europe. Lawsuits will be filed in U.S. federal courts by 2031, as a result of weather manipulation.

14

GOVERNMENTS

Crime

In-home incarceration of prisoners will be in place and being tested by the year 2015. This will be a program where prisoners are expected to restrict their movements to within their house or workspace.

Prisons will be obsolete except for the most hardened criminals or repeat offenders by the year 2050. As part of the prison eradication system, new types of step-down facilities will be constructed, and a new system of behavior modification will be instituted beginning around 2016-2017.

These reconditioning programs will be addressing cause and effect, and the development of personal self-esteem, combined with new kinds of mood-altering drugs, a professional educational program, and tracked/enforced employment systems.

Human identification and tracking (HIT) systems will be in place by 2025. These systems will be reliant on human DNA codes, and will enable positive body identification, regardless of exterior changes or modifications to look, size, weight, etc.

Institutions will be established in all fifty states in support of victims of crime by the year 2030. Crime victims will become the focus instead of the criminals. Under these new systems and approaches, society at large will accept full responsibility for the victims' losses, and ensure that criminals are dealt with fairly.

The condemnation of prisoners to death row will be officially abolished in all states by the year 2022. This will be as a direct result of studies instituted around 2004. These studies will more than suggest that there is an error rate in the determination of guilt for major crime that exceeds 21 to 25 percent. This will be found to apply in at least 14 percent of the cases of those "supposed" felons who were put to death, but were never actually guilty of the crime for which they were condemned.

The only time that death will be considered an option will be in the case of multiple murders, wherein the person convicted of the crime has requested it over long-term incarceration.

Diplomacy

A fifty-first and fifty-second state will be added to the United States before the year 2050. Neither will be Puerto Rico.

The United Nations will move to a new location outside the continental United States sometime between 2025 and 2030. This new location will probably be an island (surrounded by water on all sides.)

Russia and China will have a major disagreement over border limits sometime between 2010 and 2012. This will not result in war, but will be negotiated through a third party in an effort to avoid war.

Egypt will fully re-enter the League of Arab States in 2009.

Espionage

Being a retired U.S. Army intelligence officer, there are a lot of areas I can't discuss about our own intelligence efforts because of their relevance to actual or real capabilities.

Likewise, talking about someone else's capabilities establishes a baseline for the limits or knowns regarding those capabilities, which is also a no-no.

However, since the United States government feels that using the paranormal is of no real consequence in the collection of intelligence material(s), I will confine my comments to the paranormal aspects of such intelligence gathering.

First and foremost, because the government doesn't think there is "much to this paranormal thing" doesn't make it so. There are in fact more than a few *other governments* who continue to pursue active programs in the paranormal. One might ask why they might be doing this.

The reason primarily lies within the same context that all other developments in history have borne out as true—to be completely innovative and succeed, you have to climb into some very unusual bathtubs, explore some very unusual places, and become immersed in some very unusual concoctions.

Within the United States there is a sort of puritanical Protestant ethic that is, and always has been, an in-your-face dissuader or minefield with regard to radical ideas and/or their development. So our government, as a system, has always positioned itself in a way that suggests that there is always a great deal of caution and conservatism being brought to the fore in what or how they might be pursuing something. This makes them look good, but almost always ends up costing us a great deal.

In spite of this attitude, by early 2006 American scientists will have their first tangible proof that psi functioning is actually occurring in the brain, and where that is happening. You can essentially think of this as a Psi Lie Detector. Hook someone up a certain way, and you will be able to tell with near 100 percent accuracy when they are reporting valid psychic information, versus inventing it.

Between 2011 and 2012, we will see biological systems being remotely affected by thought alone. This will be unique in that it will have been demonstrated on unwitting subjects, that is, subjects who do not even know they are part of the experiment. For obvious reasons, this will take place outside of the United States and, in effect, be the work of another government.

I'm not suggesting that the United States should be doing this experimentation on humans. However, I am suggesting that we should be funding it and exploring it with animals. Remote bioeffects could be the most promising medical discovery in our history; it could also be the most frightening weapon.

Techniques have already been developed for using paranormal techniques for reducing the search areas for weapons of mass destruction. These have also been demonstrated under controlled conditions, and within labs. Because research into this area has received very little interest or funding, very little is known about it, other than the fact that it can be done. Effectiveness, as a result, has ranged from as little as 20 percent to as much as 85 percent, depending on which study you might be referring to.

I predict that a government will be using remote viewing to reduce search areas for weapons of mass destruction by as much as 75 percent by the year 2008. This will be a statistically stable percentage rate, which will consistently improve a great deal over time.

By the year 2025, there will be a minimum of seven countries using gifted people for paranormal intelligence-support purposes as just one more adjunct to the use of other collection methodologies.

By the year 2035, the Central Intelligence Agency will cease to exist. Its primary reporting requirements will be assumed by the Defense Intelligence Agency (DIA). Its primary responsibilities for surveillance and other clandestine overhead will be assumed by the National Reconnaissance Office. All other overseas functions will be assumed by either the National Security Agency (NSA) for matters of communication, or specific Department of Defense service agencies as regards ground, sea, or air collection. The reason for this change will rest primarily with the Agency's inability to outline and reframe their current world mission, additional and major problems with personnel, a continued loss of confidence in their ability to meet requirements, and real-world cutbacks in funding.

Ethics

Ethics will continue to degrade within our political system until specific changes are made. The first significant change will be made by 2012, with a change in how elections are funded. Special-interest groups will be forbidden to donate funds to people running for office. Tax dollars will be allocated for supporting those candidates who can muster a sufficient number of votes (probably a preset percentage of the total voting population) during a preliminary or qualifying process.

Under a great deal of pressure from the citizens of America, changes will be made to Senate and congressional rules in 2022 that will make all Senators and Congress members subject to the same laws as all other federal employees, or citizens of the United States.

Law

New laws will be introduced by the late 2020s that will provide for stiffer penalties for those who bring frivolous or groundless lawsuits. These new laws will reduce the numbers of lawsuits that are currently tying up our courts. Determination of a groundless suit will be made by a jury of peers at the request of a judge. The findings by these juries can be appealed but only at the expense of the one who brought the suit in the first place. These changes in law will reduce suits by one-third in America. People who are determined to make a groundless suit will be subject to paying all court costs incurred by both parties, the cost of frivolous suit determination, as well as additional fines, dependent on their resources.

The laws governing manslaughter will be changed before 2030. As a result, people who kill other people with automobiles while drunk will begin to receive stiffer penalties. It will no longer be looked at as an avoidable accident; it will be looked at as criminally negligent. This will have a decisive effect on the operation of local or neighborhood bars, many of which will come under civil suit as a result.

By 2025, there will be mandatory sentencing in most states as well as under federal law for the commission of a crime using a firearm. The public will balk at the minimum sentencing established, as too harsh, which will result in new gun laws being established and passed by 2042. In effect, by 2050, the only guns that private citizens will be allowed to possess will be "smart guns," those that will not fire unless they are in the hands of a registered owner. Initially this will be accomplished by electronic chip embedded within the hand of the owner. Eventually the gun itself will recognize the palm print, firmness and style of grip, as well as the body odor (pheromones) of the owner.

By 2040, there will be agreements among most member countries of the United Nations, which establishes an agreement in law. These agreements will allow for the extradition of someone from one country to another, or in the case of disagreement between countries, to a third country, to face charges of an international matter (crime across borders). The specific crimes to which this will apply will be those that are clearly not political in nature, such as murder, grand larceny, terrorist associated crimes, and crimes that are recognized as prejudicial to the good order of the United Nations charter.

The federal government will establish a common criminal database for the use of state and local police forces before 2020. This database will be maintained by the federal justice department, and fees will be paid by local police organizations for access and use. This will be separate from the currently existing Federal Bureau of Investigation database, which for reasons of law will not be permitted access except by specific request through a state judge.

Military

The military will combine its special operations units from all services into a Joint Service Strategic Operations Task Force (JSS-OTF) by 2040. Aside from removing special operations missions from the political control of a specific service, this means the following will probably take place:

1. All special unit trained personnel who have been trained in Field Craft, Jungle, Mountain, Winter, Desert, Seal, Airborne, Ranger, Special Forces, Commando, Delta Group, or Special Operations will be consolidated under a single command.

2. The Navy will be responsible for all training in naval warfare, the Army for special unit ground tactics, and the Air Force will assume all survival training requirements (winter, desert, jungle).

3. The commander of JSS-OTF will operate directly under the Secretary of Defense and be on call to the Joint Chiefs of Staff, as well as the National Security Council.

4. All decisions to utilize members of this unit as a reactionary tool will be made at the discretion of the President.

5. The unit will be separately funded.

By the year 2050, the U.S. Navy will see an increase of 22 percent in size and budget. The Air Force will see a reduction of 20 percent in aircraft as well as personnel. The Army will see a near 30 percent reduction in personnel and heavy armaments (tracked guns, tanks, and ground support aircraft.)

The only areas that will see increases within the Army will be a new generation of intelligent helicopters, which in effect will make tanks and heavy guns near obsolete.

By the year 2008, Libya will possess nuclear mass spectrographs, operating in underground facilities, that are capable of producing a minimum of 1.5 ounces of weapons-grade enriched U-235 per day.

Multinational agreements will be made by the year 2020 that will permit shared defensive weapons development between the United States and its allies. This will permit cross-pollination of new ideas, developments, and shared resources—permanently wedding the U.S. and some of its allies to a shared defensive posture.

The immediate effect will be a significant reduction in defensive costs across the board for all participant nations—about 35 to 40 percent. Future weapons development will only take place where a peaceful or nonweapons application can be demonstrated for that same development.

By the year 2060, the United States armed forces—Army, Navy, Air Force, and Marines—will be reduced by half. However, it will be twice as effective in responding with the appropriate amount of aggression.

A long-range "Death Ray" (probably a Chemical Oxygen-Iodine Laser, or COXILLA) will be operational by the year 2010. It will be capable of frying hardened military targets at ranges exceeding 25 miles, and will be track- or wheel-mounted in a vehicle, or possibly hard-mounted inside a large cargo plane. (Note: A weapon similar to this was just recently disclosed to the public with a request for permission to test it against a satellite. The original prediction was submitted in manuscript form in August 1997.)

American and European infantry will be carrying "Death Ray" rifles by the year 2015, that will have a range in excess of 500 meters. They will not operate in the sense that a ray gun operates, but will be a combination of at least three new and current technologies. (Note: A patent was issued a month ago for what is essentially a "Star Trek Phaser."

It operates by sending a variable electrical burst down a specifically constructed beam of light that has been designed and constructed to carry the electrical charge. Set on low it will paralyze the intended target; set on high, it supposedly can kill. At present, one needs a Jeep to cart around the power supply. The above prediction was also submitted in manuscript form during August of 1997).

The U.S. infantry will be wearing a lightweight, woven body armor by the year 2020. Consisting of three layers of cloth with a special weave, it will be capable of stopping a 7.62mm NATO rifle round. Since the fiber used to make this material will be a blend of new carbon-based ceramic-silicon and polymers, it will not only protect the soldier against projectiles and shrapnel, but also against fire (heat up to 1000°F for about a minute to a minute and a half.) This added benefit will not be lost on tankers.

A new helmet liner will be molded from the same material, with a full drop-down visor that will protect the face, head, and neck areas against metal fragments and bullets, as well as flames.

By 2030, the U.S. military will be wearing camouflage that mirrors the surroundings via a weak electrical current. It will also have the capacity to change from completely opaque to completely translucent, from white to black, or varying mixtures of these colors. These suits will be excessively expensive until about 2050, when they will become available to other than special operations personnel.

By 2008, ground support helicopters will be fully stealth capable. Invisible on most radars, they will also operate almost silently at night.

By 2015, these helicopters will be so well constructed from lightweight composite armor that only a direct hit with a missile will be able to bring one down. They will possess at least eight blades and be capable of automatically shedding up to half of them when damaged, while still maintaining flight.

An automatic electromagnetic gun will be fielded sometime between 2008 and 2010. It will fire twelve to twenty rounds per minute, which is a very slow cyclic rate of fire. However, its aluminum alloy bullet, which will weigh less than a pound, will be capable of blasting a nine-inch hole through sixteen inches of steel alloy at a thousand yards. Targeted with an automatic optical laser sight, it will rarely miss its target; e.g., tanks, gun batteries, radars, trucks, aircraft, munitions dumps, bunkers, etc. It will be six feet long, weigh in the neighborhood of six hundred pounds, and be powered by an on-board (vehicular mounted) generator.

A portable and lightweight armored bunker, which is infrared and stealth protected, will be fielded in late 2013. Near-impervious to night vision equipment, heat sensors, or radar, it will be helicopter-delivered for defensive positions. To prevent use by the enemy when captured, the bunker will self-destruct unless the user resets a specific code.

By the year 2050, all U.S. weapons systems will be designed to self-destruct without a proper code entry.

By the year 2030, nonlethal weapons will be a major contributor to the battlefield. They will include a method for delivering temporary blindness to large groups, a chemical that will render runways unusable without a re-action agent (two part gasoline and diesel fuel) which won't operate an engine without an additive carried by the soldiers, glow-in-the-dark chemicals you can spray on the ground to show where someone has crossed over them, aerosols that induce a temporary nervous disorder that prevents someone from sitting still, and other things that are primarily leave-behind devices to disrupt enemy movements and reaction ability.

Politics

A small skirmish will be fought over a United States territory that wishes to become independent before the year 2040. This will result in statehood for that territory.

By the year 2030, there will be three major parties—the Democrats, the Republicans, and the American Freedom Party. Because of the changes in election laws, there will be six major parties by the 2050s.

By 2030, most voting and campaigning will be done by Internet or interactive television.

Additional buildings will be constructed within Washington, D.C., to provide for nearly twice the number of "personal assistants" to Senators and Congress members after the year 2040. The issues of government will become so complex by then, it will be a requirement.

Various cabinet members will begin to abandon their Washington, D.C. offices for other areas in the nearby suburbs of Virginia and Maryland. The first to go will be the Secretary of the Treasury; the second will be the Secretary of State. These will soon be followed by many of the foreign delegations (ambassadors and their embassies). Rising crime, a lack of space, and poor services will be to blame. The empty buildings will be reoccupied by the additional members of Congress, the Senate, and an influx of special interest groups.

Taxes

The American tax system will change dramatically before 2025. My sense is that our current system will be replaced by a value-added tax based on the utility, necessity, or luxury of items being purchased, as well as consumption. In addition, there will be an individual flat tax that will probably not exceed six percent.

Because of changes to the Social Security system, the payment of taxes will no longer be required of the individual; taxes will be paid only by the employer. Individuals will have the option of adding to this tax with voluntary donations, but only up until a specific point in time.

There will no longer be allowances for personal deductions after the year 2025. Business, on the other hand, will retain the right to deduct donations to charity, all business expenses, and overhead. The tax rate on business profit will stay fixed at 6 percent, the same as for individuals.

All business taxes will be filed electronically by the year 2025. There will be no personal tax filing required—not even on capital gains, or on profits from investments.

By 2030, the Internal Revenue Service (IRS) will be cut to a third of what it is today. IRS agents will require a degree in business accounting, and at least six years of field experience running tax accounts for businesses. They will have to answer directly to a civilian oversight board in their state, as well as at the federal level.

Schools

Our schools will be our single greatest focus from the present until the year 2020. Interest will grow very slowly but steadily over the next five years.

Eventually, by 2050, nearly all public schools, kindergarten through twelfth grade, will have new buildings, new materials, and a new curriculum. Until then, there will be a very strong movement back to privately run schools.

By 2022, the average high school curriculum will no longer be recognizable. Many of the courses presently taught in the first year of college will be taught in most high school tenth-grade classrooms.

By the year 2021, the average college education will be prohibitively expensive for anyone below the upper middle class. Over half the students attending colleges within the United States will be foreign, and here on a school visa.

Government research grants to colleges will nearly double by the year 2040, as will scholarships from supporting businesses, none of which will make it any easier for students trying to get into most of the colleges in America.

There will be drastic reductions in the number of students studying law and medicine. These professions will not be well paid or respected the way they are today. The schools of choice by 2015 will be primarily the engineering departments, followed very closely by the information/computer science areas.

One of the major Ivy League Schools in the Northeast will suffer a severe shock from an exposé that will all but destroy the reputation of the school sometime between 2019 and 2022. It will involve drugs (methamphetamine), sex for money, and wife trading among the professors—to include the dean. There is a lot of gray in the colors of this school, but I don't know if this is allegorical or not.

War

There is war brewing. Within five years, 1998 to 2003, there will be a second war in northern Iraq. It will probably be much bigger than the one in which Iraq was soundly defeated in 1991 by a coalition effort in what is now known as the Persian Gulf War.

As much as I would like to state otherwise, the world will continue to be filled with tribal disputes, large amounts of military hardware, and exotic weapons systems. There are plenty of two-bit dictators still running around who lack a conscience. Power, even power that isn't real, seems to ride the crest of their desires.

In 1986, I began talking about a great Middle Eastern war that would occur within six years. I made this prediction in numerous presentations I gave at The Monroe Institute, in Virginia. Simultaneously, I was predicting that this would only be the warmup for a more significant war that would follow, probably within nine to eleven years.

Since 1991, Saddam Hussein has been rebuilding his forces. He has modified his rockets for longer range, improved his armor, and changed his tactics significantly. Even military training within Iraq has now been restructured to address what he views as his earlier mistakes. His internal security forces have been thoroughly screened and vetted, and he is now moving inexorably toward the next confrontation. He is looking for war.

The natural question is *why?*

It has to do with a number of issues. Like most self-centered dictators, he has always viewed himself as the one designated by history to change the face of his world. But this isn't the only reason. It also has to do with money and power.

Few know that to the north of Iraq lies what might be the largest natural oil reserve on the face of the planet. It rests within a square that is probably 250 x 250 miles, an area presently occupied by the extreme eastern and south-eastern tip of Turkey, the northern tip of Iran, a large portion of Armenia, and the southern half of Azerbaijan. It is an area occupied by the Kurdish people, refugees from all of these countries. It is an area that is predominantly Muslim, and clearly is an area that is very unstable.

There is a belief, and probably rightly so, that whoever controls the flow of oil within the Middle East controls much of Western Europe, and many of the now disenfranchised countries previously known as the Eastern Bloc. A war, any war, will essentially bring the primary oil-producing countries in the Middle East to a standstill. The leaders of Turkey, Iran, Iraq, Armenia, Azerbaijan, Saudi Arabia, Kuwait, and Syria know this.

Saddam Hussein also learned a number of valuable lessons from the Persian Gulf War. He now knows that aligning his forces and placing his armor, air power, missiles, and communications in fixed locations is a big mistake. He knows that waiting for an opposing military buildup is also a big mistake. He knows that Allied or NATO requirements are limited in places from which they can launch their planes, that armor is heavily affected by terrain, and that the American and European people have a false sense of strength, as a result of what most perceived to have been an easy first victory. Most of all, he knows just how precarious the balance of power is within the region, as a result of internalized conflicts in most of the adjoining states.

A new war will probably begin with Iraq invading north-western Iran. Ostensibly, it will do so under the guise of reacting to the actions of Kurdish rebels. (Iraqis call them terrorists.) Simultaneous to that action, Saddam will attempt to prod the Israelis to action with the use of a couple of long-range SCUDs carrying biological and chemical warfare agents. If the Israelis respond, and I've no doubt they will, so then will Syria, creating a war on two fronts.

The Iranians will not sit idle. They too will respond as an excuse to both occupy territory and to answer the Kurdish threat.

There will be additional surprises. Insurrection within Albania, Azerbaijan, and Turkey will soon follow.

Turkey, embroiled in internal conflict and concern over its southern border, will prompt Greece to attempt to secure its disputed territories along the Turkish borders to the north, and war will again break out on the island of Cyprus. Jordan and Saudi Arabia will initially attempt restraint, but their own internal situations will allow them very little latitude regarding the actions they take. They will be forced to take sides to prevent civil war within their own borders.

Western Europe, faced with immediate oil shortages, will not be long in joining the fray. Also, as a result of shortages and due to our commitments to NATO as well as to Israel, America will be forced to respond as well. The problem will then be exacerbated by the Western power's inability to land troops, equipment, and supplies within the region.

In all probability, Iran and Iraq will be allied in this war, further complicating a Western reaction to the conflict. The entire Middle East will be very unstable at the beginning of the conflict.

How long will the conflict last? My sense is that it will occupy the better part of four years, with perhaps another two years to reach a peace accord. The oil-rich area to the north will see substantial border changes, affecting Syria, Turkey, Iraq, Iran, Albania, and Azerbaijan. There will be no clear winners.

There will be penalties as a result of this war. Governments will change in Syria, Israel, Saudi Arabia, Jordan, Iraq, Albania, and Azerbaijan. Western Europe will become dependent on oil supplies from the United States and Russia. The NATO alliance will suffer greatly, nearly dissolving under the pressures that will be brought to bear. Following the war, insurrection will occur in countries adjacent to the area; new alliances will be formed. The Middle East will not stabilize until the year 2030. A grim future, but in all probability an accurate one.

What can be done to prevent this from occurring?

The United States and the rest of Western Europe need to ride Saddam Hussein like a horse. Iraq needs to be scoured twice over for weapons of mass destruction. When we are absolutely sure these kinds of weapons are no longer available to him, we may be able to keep him in the box.

Between 1998 and 2003 or 2004, the United States will be faced with probably the single greatest threat humanity has ever known, the possibility that one of its enemies will attempt to use a biological weapon (BW) inside the United States.

The United States has been under an executive order declaring a national emergency since the latter part of 1994, which warns of just such an event. A biological strike on an American city is no longer imminent—it's *going* to happen—they just don't know when.

There are probably a minimum of twenty-seven countries that currently have and are developing stockpiles of biological weapons. Note, I am not talking about chemical weapons here, such as mustard gas, chlorine gas, or the neurological agents that might have affected our troops during the Gulf War, but highly concentrated and specifically engineered lethal strains of virus or anthrax that are nontreatable and very quick acting. Most of these designer BW agents cannot even be decontaminated from infected areas, and no one knows how long their shelf life might be.

If a BW agent is used on an American city, there is no doubt in my mind that America will retaliate with a tactical nuclear strike. Whoever uses a BW agent on us will pay dearly for it. The problem is that this may result in far worse repercussions.

If this situation does not arise by 2004, the probability of it happening will be reduced by a percentage point with each passing year thereafter.

To counter this threat, the United States Government will have secretly ratified changes to our laws that will reinstitute and permit foreign assassination as a counterterrorist tool. This has probably already been done.

A country in the Middle East will suffer a biological warfare accident, resulting in the death of nearly one hundred thousand people, and the permanent abandonment of a large city, before the year 2001.

It is likely that civil war will break out in both Yemen and Djibouti before the year 2000.

War or no war in the Middle East, there will be civil war in Saudi Arabia before the year 2002.

The United States will withdraw troops from the Korean DMZ following the signing of peace accords in the year 2000. Within one year of the removal of troops, there will be war between North and South Korea (2001-2002).

Peace

There will be no complete peace on the planet until well into the twenty-third century.

15

SOCIAL

Anthropology

Fossilized human remains will be discovered in southeastern Syria in 2008-2009, which will establish that humankind developed an artistic capability, e.g., jewelry making, painting, statues, etc., 100,000 years earlier than currently believed.

Additional premodern human artwork will be found in caves in Australia by the year 2016 to 2017. This will confirm creativity in humankind approximately 175,000 to 325,000 years earlier then originally thought.

By the year 2010, new bone discoveries in Africa will establish that while both Neanderthal and modern man had the capacity to make tools, use fire, produce speech, and interact with one another, each is descendent from a separate line of ancestors. In other words, there is no branching of a common ancestral tree. It will take an additional seventy-five years to determine the probable origin of modern man, which will eventually be blamed on comet (ice-and spaceborne) viruses.

Archaeology

Within the next three years, a search team will discover a sealed vault-type room within seventy-five yards of the front left of the Egyptian Sphinx. Inside they will find a segment of old leather, possibly from a shoe; bits of cloth; remnants of weaving (possibly from the seat of a chair); fragments of unidentifiable clay pots or shards from plates; sand; dirt; and other debris. The most valuable object to be extracted from this room will be the air within it.

I believe the significance of the Sphinx is allegorical. It is the protective lion of Egypt. As protector of the desert sands for thousands of years, its life's blood is represented by the Nile River. Therefore, the Sphinx should be viewed in the larger sense, as though straddling the Nile with its head facing north, spilling forth the great Nile Delta from its mouth. Its paws would then be seen more as protective, covering the Sinai to the northeast, the Eastern (Arabian) Desert to the southeast, the great Western (Libyan) Desert to the southwest, and the left paw would then rest squarely over the city of Alexandria.

While the long-lost treasure of knowledge, which everyone seeks and has been predicted to be buried physically near the Sphinx, it is more likely somewhere in or near Alexandria. This will be verified between the years 2030 and 2033, with the discovery of a great tomb of clay tablets in the southeastern portion of Alexandria.

New evidence that North America was visited as early as 1100 will be discovered in Nova Scotia before the year 2022.

Evidence that the Mediterranean Sea was actually a series of lakes, much like the Great Lakes in North America, will be established before 2005.

The lost city of Atlantis will be found between 2012 and 2014. It lies in the Aegean Sea, somewhere below the water south of the city of Piraeus, Greece. The island town of Aíyina carries evidence of its existence.

Arts

A cave with hundreds of missing works of art will be discovered in the northern Alps sometime between 2008 and 2009. It will be part of the loot stolen during World War II.

Dismantled segments of the original "Amber Room," along with other valuable art pieces and treasures, will be found buried in Russia sometime between 2008 and 2010. These things will be discovered within the walls of an old Coptic church, under a woman's grave that is marked with the comment "My lovely dark Lady." Unfortunately, I have been unable to identify the town, but I believe it is within 200 kilometers of Saint Petersburg.

An unknown work by Michelangelo will be authenticated in Florence, Italy, before the year 2020. It will be found within a church.

Education

American high schools will be totally restructured by the year 2015. Students will be able to choose the days and hours they attend class. The curriculum will be altered to permit technical or trade study rather than college preparation. In effect, high school will become the apprentice period for trades such as plumbing, heating and air conditioning, electrical contractor, etc.

The competition for entry into a state college in America will be worse than it has ever been by the year 2019. The SAT scores will no longer matter, since everyone will be near maxing them. In all probability, entry will be governed by lottery.

Action will be taken by 2021 to limit foreign student attendance of American colleges. The reason so many foreign students will want to go to American colleges is twofold: there are fewer foreign advanced educational facilities, which means they are nearly always overcrowded, and as expensive as American colleges will be, they will still be cheaper than facilities overseas.

There will be at least two major strikes by teachers in American schools before 2010, primarily over the issue of salary. The average teacher will be receiving less than half what the average school administrator receives in salary or benefits.

Entertainment

By the year 2006, you will be able to purchase a television/computer screen that can be molded to a wall surface. These screens will range in size from 35 to 90 inches diagonal, with designer edges or no edges, depending on your personal taste.

Holographic—suspended three-dimensional—presentations will be possible by 2050. These will be accomplished using ionized gas chambers shaped like very large, clear-glass tubes, and the projection of intersecting energy beams. Believe it or not, this advance will be born out of an area of medical research used to fight cancers.

All television shows will be interactive by 2020.

Major feature-length movies will no longer be shot on film by the year 2030. They will be stored and manipulated digitally. Directors will be able to modify scenes after they have been shot by moving actors around in them, altering their actions, or dropping and adding lines of dialogue.

By 2075, actors will no longer be required to perform their roles. They will simply be modeled and inserted into programs that will automatically turn plots (screenplays) into movies. Making movies the old-fashioned way (digitally) will be considered very risqué, and these films will become very popular with the jet set.

To shop for books in the year 2025, you will first read about them on an electronic book sales line. Once you have made a choice, you will have the option of buying it in one of several formats. From cheapest to most expensive, these will be:

Price	Style of Book
Cheapest	An abbreviated version on computer disk
Moderate	Full version on computer disk
Expensive	Full version printed on very thin paper and trade bound

Price	Style of Book
Very expensive	Full version printed on quality paper with binding of choice

Books will no longer be printed unless ordered and the normal turnaround will be approximately two days.

By 2030, all magazines will be offered electronically on line. By 2040, it will be illegal to print magazines on paper stock.

In 2010, most journalistic matter available electronically will be automatically encrypted with a hidden string or code. Attempts to change or modify the content of the article, manuscript, book, etc., will result in garbling the entire document, rendering it unreadable. Attempts to copy the material will result in its destruction.

Before 2025, the data for most books will be stored on small plastic disks the size of a nickel. Collectors will be able to store their libraries inside small notebooks like stamps. Book readers will be able to read these books using small machines that transmit the information over an infrared connection to a pair of dark goggles.

By 2030, interactive books will work in the same way. A machine will transmit a textbook to individual pairs of goggles in a classroom, as well as a large screen on the wall. The teacher will be able to physically write on the screen, or use an electronic pointer to help students understand what they are seeing. Students will be able to take the day's lesson home with them on recorded "nickels" to study for exams.

Families

Formal extended-family living will become a significant part of American life during the next twenty-five years. People will eventually develop a preference for living in what I call "shared life centers."

As an example, three families will come together and build a home that essentially consists of three separate houses, all interconnected with common living spaces. Each family will have its private space, but will share meals, entertainment, gardening, hobbies, etc.

SHARED SPACE - MATURE ADULT LIVING

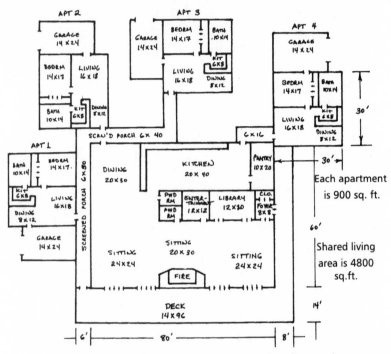

All Units are designed to accomodate the handicapped

This kind of arrangement will be appealing for the consolidation of support, both social and financial, it provides. These social structures will begin with older couples whose children have moved away. This will offer a way to reduce the burden of living alone in old age. People will be able to help one another when needed, while preserving the quiet and serenity of private living. Eventually it will spread to younger generations and families with kids, as a means of dealing with all the pressures of modern living.

Holidays

The average number of vacation days in 2025 will be twenty-one per year; average workdays, four per week.

The average number of vacation days in 2050 will be sixty per year; average workdays, three per week.

The average number of vacation days in 2075 will be none; average workdays, none. Work and play will be the same thing.

By the year 2038, Sunday will no longer be a day of rest. It will be treated just like any other day in the week.

Language

The common language for most countries in 2030 will be English. By 2075, nearly everyone will consider English their first language and their native language as secondary, to be used only for private communications.

By 2075, English will not sound the way it does today. There will be approximately forty-five recognized dialects of English, some of which will be nearly indecipherable to most English-speaking people.

Almost a third of all other languages will contain English words or phrases by the end of the twenty-first century. This will be a result of the "techno" revolution that will create whole new social systems between 2080 and 2090.

Sex

You will be able to have your physical sex changed by 2260. This will include hormonal responses, most physical characteristics, and voice alteration. The change will be undetectable.

Between 2015 and 2020, members of a medical sex clinic somewhere in Western Europe will be arrested for genetic manipulation of unborn children. Their goal? To produce a supply of hermaphrodite children to Middle Eastern brothels.

A very large push to eliminate child pornography in the Americas will begin by the year 2009. It will be kicked off by the disclosure of a large kidnapping ring that has been operating in the northeastern United States and Canada for over thirty years.

Husbands with multiple wives, and wives with multiple husbands, will be permitted in all fifty states by the year 2040, provided they agree to limit the number of children they produce.

The single greatest number of deaths will be due to sexually transmitted diseases by the year 2040.

An AIDS vaccine will be discovered before the year 2004.

The cure for AIDS will elude science until the year 2033.

By 2010, a pill will be available to men that prevents pregnancy in women.

Regardless of the moral arguments, abortions will be legal throughout the next century. In fact, as populations continue to grow out of control and we exceed our ability to feed the hungry, they will become a moot point.

Permanent castration will be a legal option for child molesters and rapists in 2010. They will be applied under the law for two-time offenders.

Sports

There will be a backlash between 2011 and 2013 to some of the growing excesses in sports. This will generate changes over a twenty-year period that will shake "sports" to the core. Some of the expected changes include the following:

1. The elimination of professional boxing, full-contact martial arts, and wrestling by 2025.

2. Maximum ceilings on a player's salary in any sport by 2015. This will begin with baseball, then quickly spread to football and basketball.

3. Maximum gate charges for attendance, by 2015.

4. Major rule changes in football, ice hockey, and other contact sports to reduce unnecessary injury, by 2022.

5. Sometime between 2006 and 2010, the introduction of a formal book of ethics with which all players will have to comply, or lose the privilege to play. These rules of ethics will also levy heavy fines.

A new type of long-distance, cross-country car racing will be introduced sometime between 2001 and 2003. It will require a team to cover a set distance within the least amount of time, and be limited to a set amount of supplies (tires and gasoline.) Vehicles taking part will have to pass certain design requirements for safety. They will have to carry two passengers—a co-driver and navigator/technician. All repairs will have to be made by the riders.

By the year 2015, the most popular sport on television will be "treasure hunts." Teams will compete to figure out clues, find other clues, and locate pre-hidden treasures somewhere in the world. The search will require participants to hike in the wild, swim rivers, climb mountains, negotiate heavy traffic, talk their way into businesses, and negotiate trades. In short, they will have to be prepared to deal with all sorts of difficulties, both mental and physical. The prize will be worth it—a minimum of one million dollars tax free.

General Social

A new material for clothing will be unveiled in the 2030s. It will have memory. When it is put on, it will automatically interact with body heat to conform to the body shape of the wearer. For those who are shape conscious, there will be material with extra padding in the right places.

A new science will exist by the year 2006. It will specifically addresses the future. The scientists who specialize in it will be called "vaticinationists." Their primary concern will center on the evaluation of the impact of current-day conceptualizing and how it might affect the future. The science will not gain sufficient prominence or have a broad effect on world decisions until after 2028. By then, it will be apparent that changes in one aspect of social behavior have decisive effects on unrelated fields of endeavor.

There will be a major resurgence in private clubs by the beginning of the next century—2001 through 2003—with membership based primarily on income. Their existence will be tested in court, but the right to form such clubs will be upheld.

16

TECHNOLOGY

Computers

By 2010, a single light fiber, half the diameter of a human hair, will be capable of carrying a million GBPS (Gigabits per second), a transmission equal to approximately 100 million voice channels.

In 2035, scientists will construct a "Quantum Computer System" capable of solving "multistate" problems that otherwise would require an excessive amount of time and equipment. What will actually contribute to the creation of this new device will be new mathematical and algorithmic theories in programming that will come into existence ten years prior to the machine's existence.

Hard-disk computer storage systems will be replaced in 2008 with electromagnetic/chemical storage systems. These will mimic the way "memory cells" currently operate within the human brain. Changes in the "stored" state will be achieved by electromagnetically altering the chemical makeup of molecule chains. This will result in a quantum leap in speed as well as in the amount of information that can be stored and retrieved. The older technologies (nickel-sized disks) will be relegated to permanent storage requirements instead of dynamic.

A special-purpose computer processor chip called a "Cascade Chip" will be introduced between 2024 and 2025. Its primary purpose will be in support of robotics. When married up with "jell-like" chemical memory agents, it will allow new artificial intelligence operations not available at this time.

Advances in computer design will continue to flourish between now and the year 2050, providing unbelievable increases in memory, power (speed), and communications capability.

By 2050, computer memories will experience a fiftyfold increase, with a fivefold reduction in size. Beginning in 2005 with a multicolored/multifrequency recording technology, the expected norm will be a transfer of data through dual-switch processors at 1 megabyte per 8 nanosecond rates or faster from disk to processor.

Floppy disks will be replaced with hard disk drives using removable and rewritable disks one-third the size of today's hard CDs by 2008. The standard RAM on the average machine will be 128 MB, with 256 MB the industrial standard on business machines (all on a single plug-in module.)

In the year 2015, most home computers will be interfacing with the Internet through a newly developed telephone relay system that will operate at three times current ISDN speeds. This will help eliminate some of the current communication problems, which will worsen through the year 2019 and cause computer operators to continue to vacillate between hard lines and satellites.

By 2025, there will be over 600 million Internet users in homes and businesses throughout the world. By then, the Internet will be operating mostly through up-/down-link satellites and roof-mounted dishes about the size of current home visual systems in use today—in both directions. By then, satellite systems will finally be favored over hard wires.

By 2025, all software will be voice-activated and controlled, eliminating the need for keyboards and the mouse. Software will only recognize the voice of the owner and act as an integral part of the computer security and firewall system.

All computers will have full fax, data, voice, and moving picture transfer capabilities built into the motherboard by

2005. Use of the phone as a communications device will be nearly eliminated, resulting in higher fees for computer linkups and usage.

By 2010, most phone companies will be offering flat-rate fees for all services, which will average $60 a month regardless of usage or distance.

By the end of 2050, the average home computer will have 1000 times the current processor power, being equal to about eight times the current supercomputer operating capacity. They will operate at room temperature with interlaced quad-processors of ten megabytes each. Internalized communications within the box itself will be based on optic fibers and light links. All of the hard connections will be severed, with all links to printers, keyboards, plotters, etc., by burst, extreme high-frequency wideband broadcast methods.

By 2011, computers will be required in all elementary schools. Courses in information accessing will be taught at all high schools, and college students will be expected to use computers and the Internet for all their research, report writing, and dissertations by the year 2020. As a result, they will also be tested on their ability to root out fact from fiction.

By the year 2020, there will be a substantial rift between computer-literate and computer-illiterate social levels within American society, as well as within other countries. This will have a decisive and very negative effect on wages, employment, schooling levels, and competition in the job market, which will further result in an increase in negative social pressures and declining attitudes. Deliberate acts of violence against computer system facilities will rise dramatically.

Engineering

A new home sound system will be unveiled by one of the leaders in the sound industry between 2002 and 2004. It will produce sound that is controlled by computer to simulate

360-degree surround sound, or 3-D sound simulation. The computer will use sensors to detect how many people are in the room and where they are located in comparison to the shape of the room and the furniture in it. It will then alter the sound being emitted from ten or more speakers, changing their wave fronts to give an impression that one is always standing in the middle of an orchestra pit.

By the year 2010, most newly constructed homes in the United States and Western Europe will have seasonal, self-regulated window glass that will bring more light into a room during winter months, and less during the summer. This will result in a minimum reduction in home energy consumption of 20 to 30 percent. The technology will also bring about major changes in building construction, allowing for the use of glass as a roofing material throughout the home, and self-darkening walls made from glass for bedrooms. You'll be able to regulate when you can or can't see through the walls, which will also increase security.

Medicine

By the year 2006, synchronized x-ray particles will permit cell-by-cell pictographs of most cancer growths within the human body. This, along with computer tomography, will allow for the destruction of cancer cells with tumor-specific radiation treatments in hard-to-reach places. These techniques will minimize damage to surrounding healthy tissue cells. In effect, the computer-driven x-ray device will destroy each cell of a tumor by having memorized its actual location within the other cells of the body.

Within ten years (1998 through 2008), there will be a silver bullet cure for most cancers, as well as the development of a vaccine for AIDS.

By 2010, surgeons will be performing complex micro and macro operations without having to break the skin of the patient. They will be doing this with a whole range of electromagnetic tools that operate in the same way as normal tools. These specialists will be able to perform some types of internalized surgery by using magnetic resonance imaging in conjunction with powerful high-speed computers, narrow-spectrum particle beam generators, and incidence trajectory, to vaporize, cauterize, or alter internal organ cells. By 2020, they will be using modifications of these machines to eradicate narrowing of the arteries (on an emergency basis only—because by then this will normally be done with intravenous), internal eye repair, and radical brain surgery.

Contrary to some of the bad news in previous chapters, there will be great strides in medicine. They will be slowed somewhat by the economic crunch, but it is because of that crunch that many successes will take place. Those of us in the West will have to begin looking at alternative methods of healing that are cheaper and more readily available.

The vaccine developed for AIDS won't be a complete cure, but it will nearly arrest the AIDS disease. Most of those who contract AIDS will be able to live full and productive lives without the debilitating effects. This significant discovery will center on a natural defense that can be keyed or initiated within the AIDS virus itself, through genetic manipulation. Unfortunately, the discovery will bring a new set of problems that will begin to emerge sometime just prior to the year 2025.

By 2035, we will lose our current lines of defense against the common flu. There will be a major epidemic sometime near that time frame, during which tens of thousands will perish. This will prompt the discovery of a completely new technology for addressing the antibiotic requirements of humankind. It will probably also be based on a form of genetic manipulation a step removed from that devised to address the AIDS problem. What is most interesting here is that the method developed will essentially simulate the AIDS virus, only in this case, it will have a positive effect.

By the year 2020, a new understanding about healing and medicine will be born out of increasing problems within the health care system. Inpatient care at a hospital facility will be viewed as necessary only in the most severe of cases. People will be encouraged to seek out alternative means to deal with chronic pain or common ailments. Herbs and diet will be recognized as having the most significant impact on preventative medicine. Outpatient programs for preventative medicine will expand five-fold in that period of time.

A completely new approach will be developed with regard to surgery. Medications will be developed between now and the year 2025 that will in effect reduce the necessity for open-heart, pancreatic, thyroid, gall bladder, or other forms of organ surgery to less than 15 percent their current levels. The preferred form of surgery (any surgery) will be microscopic, or in the least invasive way possible. As a result, most surgery, even the most radical, will be done on an outpatient basis by the year 2035.

Just before 2020, a teaching hospital somewhere in the central Atlantic states will discover that two "practices" customary in current surgical procedures have actually been responsible for nearly a third of the deaths during surgery over the past twenty years. It will be something simple—like the kind of plastic wrap used to store sterile instruments, or cotton fibers—but a major cause of complication (shock to the system).

By the year 2025, forms of patient-selected suicide will be openly discussed as an option for those with terminal diseases or who are beyond the age of sixty-five. It will take an act of Congress, as well as a U.S. Supreme Court decision to validate a person's right to die—which will take place sometime in the year 2020. Most of the philosophic arguments "pro right to suicide" will be based on future findings that support a belief in life after death and reincarnation (or multiple incarnation states). Surprisingly, most of these arguments will be theologically based.

By 2030, neutral DNA tissue will be specifically engineered and grown for transplant purposes. At first, the tissues will be used for plastic surgery and cosmetics. Custom or designer replacement body parts, based on the DNA of the intended recipient, will be available by the year 2040.

By the year 2020, new molecular-neuro/electrical chip transmitters will be developed that will be capable of transmitting across breaks in human nerve fibers. Although they will only be able to demonstrate gross muscle motor control at first, by the year 2035, molecule-sized transmitters will be implanted under the skin to transmit and activate portions of the body that have previously been deficient as a result of major nerve damage or trauma.

There will be semi-permanent makeup (cosmetics) by the year 2015. Once applied it will remain in place until a chemical debonding agent is used to remove it. The makeup will be impervious to body oils, water, wind, perspiration, or almost any agent other than the specifically designed debonding agent.

A cosmetic that can change the color of your skin will be available in pill form by the year 2025.

Nuclear Weapons

A new form of nuclear weapon will be demonstrated by the year 2030. It will use plutonium as a detonator, and antimatter stored within an electromagnetic bottle as a source of fuel.

Its radioactive contamination, size relative to previous weapons, and visible fireball will be much smaller than ever seen before. However, its destructive power will be awesome—easily a thousand times its equivalent size in older technology.

A primitive nuclear weapon (suitcase bomb) will be taken from a terrorist organization in Western Europe sometime between 2009 and 2011. Its actual destination will have been the United States.

Power

Expect a big increase in brownouts by between 2015 and 2020. The primary problem will be aged and worn-out equipment and infrastructure. People living in the South will be the most affected, and can count on new regulations on power usage. Repairs and equipment replacement will extend well into 2115.

The first operational fusion device to produce usable electricity will become operational between 2030 and 2035. Its initial energy output will be 35–40 percent above the energy required to sustain itself. It will be based on a completely new technology than exists today, one that suggests a different approach to electromagnetic containment.

Efficiencies in the transfer of electrical power from solar collectors to storage systems will quadruple by the year 2009. This will be accomplished through the creation of new plastic-metal films, constructed by combining a high-charge-carrying molecular metal with a high-temperature electromagnetic conductor. The substantial increase in efficiency will make the use of solar energy more financially acceptable to the person on the street.

Telecommunications

By the middle of the next century, we will no longer be communicating by phone. Computers and virtual reality will make it possible for those with a lot of money to relax in a comfortable chair and talk to someone, regardless of distance, just as though they were sitting across the room. Those without a lot of money will be wearing a set of goggles that give the impression of standing in front of the individual to whom we are speaking.

A portable communications device will probably be worn on the wrist and look very much like a watch by

2035. It will be powerful enough and smart enough to interact by voice commands. No matter where we might be standing, it will notify us of a call, to which we will be able to respond. The exchange might go something like the following:

Device:	You have a caller, Sir.
Joe:	Connect. (My wife's face appears on the dial.)
Joe:	Hi, Sweetie.
Wife:	Pick up some of those carrot burgers on the way home tonight.
Joe:	OK. See you soon.
Wife:	Love.
Joe:	Love.
Joe:	Break. (Screen vanishes.)

We will also be able to interact with people in the office, or our boss (the actual machine that runs it). We'll be able to connect with the other intelligent machines in our life, such as our personal transporter or our house. We could tell the transporter where to collect us and it would show up there on its own, or maybe have the house check up on the kids:

House:	Kids are in their rooms studying at the moment, Sir. (Yeah, right.)

By the year 2050, these machines will be so powerful and have capabilities that are so much greater than our best and brightest computers today, we'll wonder how we ever got along without them. "User friendly" will have a whole new meaning by the end of the next century.

Spaceships

By the year 2025, we will be flying into and out of space in a plane very much like today's Concorde. The only difference will be that it will carry much larger payloads and a lot more passengers. A discovery that will make this possible will be made on the research-oriented space station.

One of the first things we will learn to do in the near vacuum of space is to grow new metal alloys that have crystal orientations not possible in metals formed on Earth. The crystal properties will allow for the creation of new engines and skins for our planes, which will be able to dissipate huge amounts of heat from reentry and atmospherics. These new metals will also have some interesting stability advantages with regard to electronics and how we are able to run things.

The first spaceship to Mars will be constructed in orbit by the year 2050. The engine will be an atomic hybrid, capable of pulse drive, and will propel the ship to Mars in a record four months or less. The crew will land on the surface in a gliderlike plane with a wing construction similar to a very large parasail. A small but very dependable solid-fuel rocket will bring them back to the ship. Once the uniqueness of the first trip wears off, there will be at least six more trips to Mars within a ten-year period. A station will be built on the planet's surface before 2075. We will find that we have the ability to produce our own construction materials, oxygen, and water from elements present on the planet. Most of the station will actually be constructed underground.

Why go to Mars?

Research mostly. The first three visits to Mars we will bring back a minimum of six new alloys, and at least one addition to the periodic table of the elements. We will also confirm that at one time, a million years earlier, there were other humanoids that visited Mars and died there.

By the year 2080, we will be producing almost as much power on the edge of space as all the nuclear reactors operating on Earth today (in 1998). We will beam most of this power back to the surface for use in our factories and to heat cities in winter.

By the end of the twenty-first century, we will truly be "children of the stars."

17

THE YEAR 3000

If we survive to the year 3000, and I have not yet encountered a truly valid reason why we shouldn't, I perceive a world that is literally covered with bioscapes.

I see large sections of very old-growth trees where trees have never existed before. There are manicured fields stretching as far as the eye can see, deliberately laced and folded together with large hedgerows of trees, parks and gardens dividing the fields.

It is a place where the diversity of plants far outweighs the needs of the masses, and the needs of nature are being honored instead of abused.

Jutting up from this abundant background of green, brown, and yellow are brand-new cities. Almost without exception, they are located inland, away from the ocean edges.

Most appear to be near circular by design. They are formed of concentric rings, with six or seven grassy, garden-covered spokes running from the center ring to the outer ring edges.

There are collections of buildings, mostly white, glimmering at the center with stubby skyscrapers interlocked. Glasslike and well-covered pedestrian raceways fill the voids between the towers, some rising as high as twenty floors above the gardens below. These city cores are much smaller than I would have expected, perhaps forty or fifty buildings in all. It is hard to tell where the base is for most of these buildings. Some seem to be embedded in the ground almost as deep as they are above it.

Cityscape

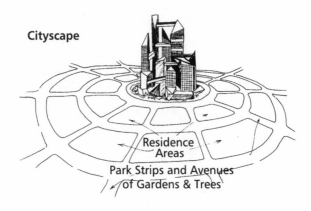

Residence Areas

Park Strips and Avenues of Gardens & Trees

Aboveground City

Cut-away view

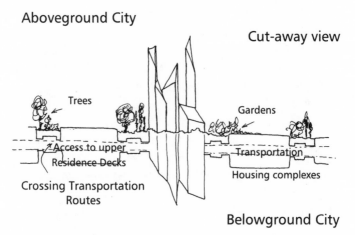

Trees

Gardens

Access to upper Residence Decks

Transportation

Crossing Transportation Routes

Housing complexes

Belowground City

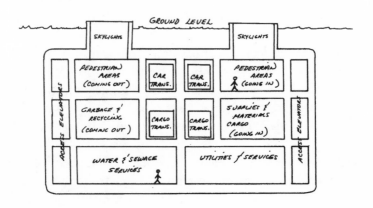

GROUND LEVEL

SKYLIGHTS

SKYLIGHTS

ACCESS ELEVATORS

PEDESTRIAN AREAS (COMING OUT)

CAR TRANS.

CAR TRANS.

PEDESTRIAN AREAS (GOING IN)

GARBAGE & RECYCLING (COMING OUT)

CARGO TRANS.

CARGO TRANS.

SUPPLIES & MATERIALS CARGO (GOING IN)

WATER & SEWAGE SERVICES

UTILITIES & SERVICES

ACCESS ELEVATORS

There doesn't appear to be a single ground level, but each of the levels seem to be particular to a specific function or design within the cities overall form.

There are no paved streets. My sense is that vehicular traffic is forbidden within the confines of these cities. The spokes and concentric circles are open spaces filled with small gardens and parks. Not a design flaw, these open spaces hide modes of public transportation well below ground. Small and silent subways are moving as if by magic through a horizontal maze of multipurpose tunnels.

In the city proper, or where the skyscrapers jut from deep within the ground, there are various connections to what appear to be primary public transportation systems that move vertically, like elevators skimming upward along the exterior skins of the buildings. Within the rings outside this area, the primary mode of movement from one level to another is by stepping onto rotating platforms.

There are also subways that follow each of the rings, providing access to other portions of the city.

Most of the residential units that are part of this city are constructed within the outer rings. The upper floors have skylights or rooftop balconies that open to the manicured gardens around them. Encased within these sections of trees and gardens, the units look like small cottages, belying the size and space of the rooms below.

The main services, such as sewer, power, communications, and water are apparently run through multipurpose tunnels used for public transportation. Also contained within these tunnels are conveyors that carry a minimum of refuge or garbage to a collection point some distance outside the city.

The average city appears to be quite small, something less than perhaps 200,000 people. Most of the cities I can see on the planet seem to be very similar in appearance. There are differences based on climate, or perhaps because of location, but for the most part they are remarkably alike.

Large industrial parks, where all manufacturing takes place, sit on the outer edges of the cities. Everything moving into or out of the city goes through these parks. There are vehicles here that load or unload products packed in containers, uniform in appearance, used to carry things into the city and elsewhere. They look a lot like the luggage carriers on aircraft today, only they float just off the ground and seem to be individually powered. They, too, move throughout the subway system.

Adjoining these industrial parks are processing facilities apparently designed for reclaiming nearly all of the waste being produced by the city.

The sewage, rather than being treated, is actually being pumped out into a large man-made swamplike area. The swamp is like a large ingress to a series of lakes and water impoundments, occupying hundreds of acres of land. Surrounding these lakes are smaller processing plants that appear to be handling fish, algae, crustacean, and other aquaculture products.

Pumping stations at the outer edges of the swamp are being

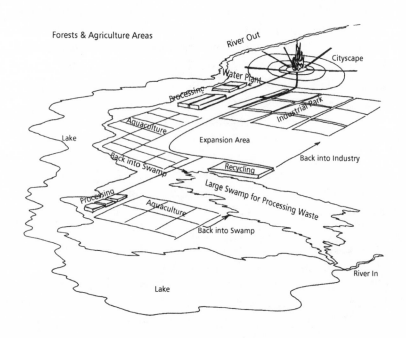

used to circulate fresh water into the swamp area itself, as well as to pump effluent out to the fields and farms beyond the city, where it is being macerated in with natural farm wastes to be used as fertilizer.

Hard waste or garbage is being processed within the industrial park area. All that can be reclaimed in terms of recycling is being done here. My sense is that most of the products that are being used are actually designed with eventual waste management in mind. It is as if things that will be used are deliberately designed and manufactured so they can be run through a recycling process at the end of their usable life.

Very little appears to require burning, water and chemicals being the preferred method for recycling.

I also have a very strong sense that most of the heat being generated by the industrial section of the city is also being used by the city for power and heat.

The primary source of heat used by the city is hard to identify, perhaps because it is being delivered by numerous methods and from several localities, as well as on some kind of a beam from above. It is probably a combination of solar and industrial in origin, with over half being some form of chemical interaction or reaction.

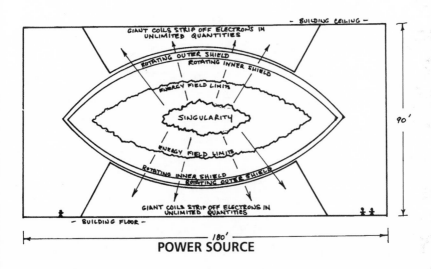

POWER SOURCE

Power is being provided by a separate facility that doesn't seem to have any operating parts—that is, no moving parts or engines. There are large cylindrical pie-shaped forms that are made of a metallic substance I've never seen before. Inside, I have an impression of electromagnetic current that keeps some form of fluid moving at a constant speed. The output of these devices is tenfold greater than the electrical requirement for keeping the fluid rotating.

Beyond the cities are small towns. They, too, are nearly perfectly circular and have no roads. Less than ten city blocks across, they are mostly residential. A few buildings within their centers appear to be miniaturized versions of the city skyscrapers. I have a sense that most of the services within these villages or towns are relegated to these buildings, much like the larger buildings in the bigger cities.

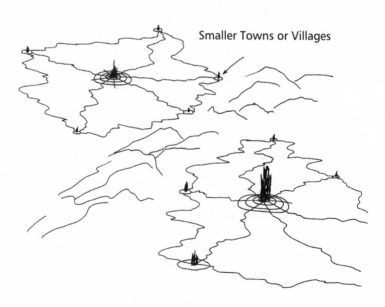

Smaller Towns or Villages

Cities are separate from one another with
Town Dependencies

There are very smooth ribbons of highways interconnecting the towns, which are all centered around the larger cities, forming clusters occupying areas of approximately 100 by 100 miles. There do not appear to be connecting highways between the city clusters. I have a sense that there is no reason for travel between the two, or if there is, it is a means of travel that is inherently invisible to the casual observer.

There are isolated buildings located here and there, throughout the woodlands between the city clusters. These appear to be quite rustic and are built to blend in gracefully with the surrounding countryside. They have the feel of resorts, but I don't believe they are run that way. My sense is that while many families can be staying at one of these facilities, they are shared or communal by nature, and are meant to support a singular function. They are places of solitude, rest, peace, and simplicity, almost like a monastery, where people go for a retreat, or to pray.

There are a few individual residences sporadically scattered between city clusters, but they, too, appear to be set aside for some special purpose. They are not family residences, but have a feel of authority about them. They are being used for something to do with government, retention or detention.

There are some differences between North American, West European, East European, African, South American, and Asian countries with regard to cities.

Within North America, the city clusters are mostly as I have described them.

West European cities are clustered in much tighter arrays. Most of the land between cities is tillable or open acreage. Forests have been relegated to mountainous or rocky and uneven ground areas. Most of the great cities along the coast have been moved fifteen to twenty miles inland, except for those occupying great harbors. The harbor cities are much smaller than they are in present time, and appear to be predominantly dedicated to the seafaring trade.

Eastern European cities are much like those found in North America, but are centralized in three primary bands: a band running north to south along the western borders of what used to be Estonia, Latvia, Belarus, and the Ukraine; a second band running north to south through what used to be St. Petersburg, Moscow, and Kiev, splitting the Black and Caspian Seas; and a third band, running from the central region of the Ural Mountains to along the northern China border.

African cities are clustered in the southern tip of Africa, as well as along the southern shores of the Mediterranean Sea. But those that were immediately on the shore, however, have moved inland approximately twenty miles.

South America remains fairly unchanged except for the slight move inland that is so much in evidence everywhere.

China is split horizontally. The upper half shows very little evidence of population. The southern half has a thick band of city clusters blending into those of India and the Southeast Asian peninsula. Japan contains only three or four city clusters, all huge in comparison to other cities throughout the world.

My sense is that the world's population, based on what I see of the cities, is only about one-sixth what it is today.

It is evident that new rules have been established with regard to energy, its production, use, and availability. There is now an unlimited supply of power. There do not seem to be any hydroelectric plants or atomic fission or fusion devices left. Nor are there large and powerful electron-storage devices required. Unlimited power seems to be a reality.

We have apparently figured out how to harness the power of the cosmos—the power of the stars.

One interesting development is that, as a result, we have also learned to alter the effects of gravity. This in turn has led to the creation of brand-new alloys, combinations of known elements into new or unknown elements, which has led to actual physical materializations. This new knowledge has permitted immense changes in the way we view and utilize other forms of transportation, communication, even how we now address disease. The power units look like huge, living machines that are capable of enormous, almost incalculable, power output.

Similar to the way we envision the elusive UFOs of today, these vibrating and focused power-generating machines exist within reality as singularities—anomalies that are capable of existing within our reality, but that are not actually subject to it. There are doorways to the universe of power just beyond the envelope of our planet. With these machines, we possess a potential for altering space/time, at least in how the machines and people directly relate to it.

The machines appear to be circular, spherical, or conical in shape and have some kind of interior movement. This probably has to do with the distribution of power within our space/time, because there seems to be a singular flow, which is always outward.

The power generated by these machines is kept local, or under control, by the balance between the reality within and without. While each machine will have the enormous power of a universe behind it, it cannot exceed itself or the space in which it sits—a cosmic check valve.

My sense is there is an action or reaction taking place at the periphery of these machines that appears as an aura or glow surrounding or enveloping them. Altering output on one side of the machine or the other results in a near-instant exchange or relocation of energy. It is conceivable that this could occur over a great distance.

Left to run unattended, or in a balanced condition, the machines generate huge amounts of electrons, which are being harnessed for whatever purpose is required. It may be for running other machines, producing unlimited heat, or supporting the surrounding industries and homes within the city. There are no limits to the machines' output, as they are only dependent on the capabilities of mechanisms used for stripping off or delivering power from the machine.

I have a sense that there has been a great religious war that ravaged the land, but it has long since ended. Only four of the larger religious sects survived. They no longer exist separately but are now considered segments of the whole. They are highly modified from their original concepts, or at least the concepts by which we judge them today. They seem quite similar in content, and are treated as such. Buddhism, Christianity, Hinduism, and Islam are now being commonly referred to as "The Guiding Principles of Spirituality," or "The Ways of Belief." They are based on a common principal, which is that once in a while the Grand Engineer (that which we currently call God) manifests a representative with an exceptional insight to spirituality. Over the centuries, this job or responsibility has been shared among a number of people (those we call prophets.)

Religion and government support the observance of specific religious holy days set aside to honor the Grand Engineer. Religion also establishes that it is far better for everyone to practice their religion, not by prayer, but through actions and deeds.

These actions and deeds are outlined within a group of manuals or writings so that we can understand them. The writings cover such things as not using intoxicating or mind-altering substances to excess; personal and family cleanliness and hygiene; acceptance of neighbors, friends, associates, even strangers as close family members; mutual respect for all others, their ideas, their space, and above all else, their differences. In other words, religion is now an everyday action. It is a common code of action and decision making in the year 3000.

There are still churches. They contain no statuary, no crosses, no candles, no low light, no religious imagery of any kind. They do appear to have certain forms of mandalas, which are used for meditative practices, as well as a form of art. These churches are generally circular, step downward toward the center, and are used more for socializing than anything else. They are bright and sunny places, with lots of glass and beautiful indoor and outdoor gardens. They are places where people seem to gather for two reasons.

First, they gather to share in meditation on holy days. The forms of meditation used are not related to prayer, but are considered necessary for becoming centered and clear about our actions. The point is to be awake and aware. People are encouraged to congregate in large groups on holy days, so that they might meditate for a brief period together. In this case, performance by example is thought to be of more value than directed teaching of any sort.

There are combined teachings of great religious leaders that people sometimes bring and read or share with others, but these types of readings are usually done in private at home, since they are more of personal taste.

I can see no evidence of the Old Testament, except a formal, museumlike place, nor do any of the primary religious writings of today exist in common hands. They are reserved only for study and historical purposes.

Over the years, religious conferences have provided guidance on which portions of the Bible, Koran, Dhammapada, Tanakh, Rig-Veda, and at least six or seven other sacred writings were of real value and should be combined within the five volumes that now comprise "The Way."

Almost without exception, the portions of text that dealt with everyday life, the treatment of others, or the treatment of oneself, were kept. Dogma addressing the past, fear, retribution, revenge, or punishment was deleted. Much of the newest writings apparently deal with focus, awareness, and the implementation of religious practice by the living of it—the obvious reason for the new documents.

Before and following the period of meditation, people appear to meet in very large groups. These are social get-togethers and are like large family gatherings. There are no religious requirements at these times other than to be friendly and open to one another. Exchanges of the vows for matrimony and the dedication of children to living a life in honor to the grand design are some of the events surrounding these holy days and church-type social gatherings. These are celebrated and supported by everyone present.

There are those among the followers of "The Way" who apparently do not support a belief in the Grand Engineer, or a God. They believe in a single unifying power that drives the cosmos they live in, but do not ascribe to the personalized vision of a creator. There are segments of writings that also integrate this belief within the basic spiritual tenets. These people are not viewed as different, only as having a different perception(s) of the same thing.

People are encouraged to use these churches at other times as well. Large gatherings like picnics, parties, or even larger social affairs, which are communal in nature, take place throughout the year in these churches. It is as though religion has become an expression of life, a way of living more than worship. It no longer emphasizes a judgment call on whether or not someone is a sinner. Caring about others and oneself and living as an example of balance within the universal law is the entire thrust of "The Way."

While "The Principles of Spirituality," or "The Way," seem to substantially represent the majority of the population, there appear to be others as well.

There are major existing cultural distinctions. Large segments of the world population have adapted their ways of living to the overall belief that religion must be demonstrated to be of any value.

Large regions share similar traits. North America and Western Europe are generally the same. Eastern Europe, including Asia, share similar cultural and spiritual aspects with one another, but South America and Africa differ from the rest. Their cultural expressions within the framework of "The Way" seem to harbor a much greater diversity. These cultural differences, whether diverse or generalized, are respected.

Smaller sects and cults that attempt to deviate from the overall consensus still exist. They vary according to the very nature of the cities in which they are present. Because they are mostly city-dependent, the groups are not large, but they are tolerated as long as the basic tenets of the over-all belief structure are being maintained—lived through example.

Most of these smaller sects and cults are either being driven by strong personalities, or are seeking something in addition to that which is expected or accepted as the norm. There are some who are using drug-induced altered states, or ritualistic prayer, as an example.

I have a sense that these small cults or groups seek direct answers to the great mysteries—such as why humankind exists—and ultimately, a more direct connection to God. These pursuits are not only tolerated by the whole, but are encouraged, as the overall consensus is that humankind has a basic natural drive to find such answers. As long as they are not disruptive to the whole, or affect society in a negative way, they are pretty much left alone.

Synods, or great meetings, are held every ten years, and are hosted by centers of religious investigation. Each region has its own major center for spiritual development, and they bring their findings to these great conventions to be discussed and shared.

All governments accept and financially support the religious requirements of local cities. They build the churches and provide for their maintenance and upkeep. Aside from the act of living the religion, and demonstrating tolerance and support, there is no other connection between government and spirituality. That seems to be enough.

One of the basic tenets that seems to come from the religious beliefs of the time is that there is a single power within the universe that has caused all matter, both inanimate and animate, to exist. It is viewed more as a "way" or "method" by which humans can be connected to each other, as well as to the creator, or the power behind creation. There is no pretension that we might ever know the face of this Grand Engineer, beyond what we see displayed within the magic of our reality.

There is a strong indication that humankind has developed a much greater understanding of the role we play in the construct of reality, and how a single purpose of being is our best protection or insight for learning most about what might affect us. In other words, we now recognize the true or universal laws that govern our reality, our place within the physical, and how our actions affect the other species within it.

There is an assumption that all other life on the planet, as well as within the universe, shares in this concept. Actions are taken from a personal, group, governmental, and planetwide viewpoint. It is understood that whatever our actions may be, they affect not only those closest to us, but have a decisive effect on life we may not even know exists. Everything is inter-connected; all of reality within our cosmos is one. Birthed from a single source, everything is related. Cause and effect is the single constant that directly affects change.

Within the community, there are keepers of the Seal, the Covenants of Agreement. They are not priests in the way we understand now, but more like protectors.

For nearly four hundred years, humankind has come to realize that science and religion are virtually the same. Actions taken in the name of science are not always the best actions, nor are those taken solely in the name of religion. None of the learned men or women who are the protectors are individually powerful enough to effect a change. However, they understand that change can be effected by the course of a society.

Their job is to be vigilant, to constantly be on the cutting edge of cultural action, which may be the cause of sudden changes to the future of humanity. They study the ethics, keep a watchful eye over knowledge, and sit in the driver's seat of progress or change for the collective.

Progress alone is no longer a reason for opening doors to a new technology. The possible impact that technology might have on the whole is viewed as a serious consequence. By the year 3000, we have a much greater understanding of how our very actions, thoughts, words, and deeds change reality as we understand it to be.

The spirituality of the future isn't perfect. Because we are human, there are still glitches and flaws. But we have apparently traveled a long way down the road of understanding, and are now standing in the doorway of conscious awareness. We seem to have a much better grasp of what that awareness can bring. It is clear that prayer is now viewed as action, and action is viewed as creation.

The population is very small. In searching for a cause, I sense that there were at least two great wars, but they were not the cause. There were terrible plagues that stripped the world—over six hundred years past—during a dark time when men created germs that would not have otherwise seen the light of day. Now population controls are voluntary and precise.

Births are planned and orchestrated according to both need and desire. Death, on the other hand, still comes as a part of life. Care is no longer taken to ensure a higher IQ, the right kind of eyes, or additional strength. Even the sex of a child is held in wonderment till birth. The only concern is health. At the moment of conception, genes are checked to ensure that the child will have every reason to expect the best of health. If a defect is found, it is corrected in the womb. Abortion is the final recourse and used only within the first two weeks of pregnancy.

Children are viewed as the future, the light of humanity. Abuse is never tolerated and all children are treated as one's own till the age of ten. Children are never seen by anyone as strangers. There are no ethnic groups. There is little variance in skin color, size, shape, color or consistency of hair, eyes, and teeth.

Children are no longer children when they pass their first decade and begin their learning in earnest. They are required to learn and possess at least two technical skills and two arts by age eighteen. They must show equal ability in all four. They learn these things through formal schooling and through mentoring with four adults of like skills.

They are taught their sexual manners by age sixteen and understand that the sharing of one's body is viewed as a spiritual act, one that should be held in some respect. All men and women are protected medically against conception by a reversible vaccine used only at the times when conception is desirable.

Beyond advisement of social functions, musicals, plays, artistic displays, and other human social interactions, there are no product advertisements because there are no products. Work is considered a privilege, an honor, by which one can provide something that is constructive for others. Everyone receives what is needed, and there is no reason to compete for sustenance. Therefore, there are no banks.

Food production and manufacturing are driven by need, and only a set rate of excess is allowed to guarantee delivery in case of an emergency. There are no retail sales, but there are skilled individuals trained to provide things, such as clothing; the cleaning, production, and delivery of food; utensils; and other necessities. There are also technicians capable of providing materials for the expression of art and other social amenities.

Bridges, buildings, forests, transportation, communication systems, etc., are held in common rather than privately.

There are security personnel available in the event of crime, which apparently still occurs. Security is not a full-time job, but one of the four skills learned, and secondary to what are considered more primary skills.

Behavioral modification for criminals is considered a primary skill. It's always conducted away from normal society, in a thoroughly isolated location. Criminals are never allowed to congregate or speak with one another, but are instead assigned mentors who see to the specifics of their modification. Their original skills are re-evaluated to see if they might be better suited to another area of training. Once their skills have been reinforced, and they have demonstrated their ability to appropriately fit in with other people, they are returned to society—but always to a different city. Behavior modification includes gene, hormone, psychiatric, and emotional therapy. Those who cannot be rehabilitated, or who fail rehabilitation more than twice, are remanded to a city where they are forced to live within certain rules, under penalty of more radical punishment.

There is no military, however there is a diplomatic corps that is responsible for monitoring agreements and treaties. Violations of the treaties or agreements between states are dealt with by a world court, consisting of seven members. Lower courts can deal with minor problems, such as arguments between people. Majority vote rules, so no court has less than three, or operates with an even number of judges. These courts are concerned with fairness at the time and place of offense, and only secondarily with set precepts of law. That means that just because a decision was made a certain way in one case, it will not always be made that way. A defendant has an automatic right to one appeal, which requires a completely different court and members.

There are no taxes, and there are no wars. The decisions of the world courts are honored by all. Apparently, that is a residual of the terrible wars of the twenty-third and twenty-fourth centuries.

There do not appear to be many differences in art, entertainment, sports, or socializing, other than the technologies involved. The greatest interest appears to focus on things that give rise to anticipation, emotional feeling, and beauty. Violence is not totally eliminated from these activities, but it is viewed as being in very bad taste when it exceeds a certain level. It is sometimes considered necessary to make a point, particularly in historical reference. It is used rarely and only when absolutely necessary to the plot or statement. A good test of skill or ability, sportsmanship, joy, beauty, and relaxation are the treasures far more sought after. Sex is a gift readily shared.

Technology is so advanced it seems almost invisible. Everything happens almost automatically. Sensors are tuned to respond to the human presence, any human presence. Voice stress, body heat or temperature, even the content of conversation is monitored by intelligent machines that then attempt to provide what might be necessary. The room temperature, air movement, ambient sounds, or music are all automatically set or changed based on how the machines read a human's presence.

Almost any command can be carried out at any location, provided the person frequents that area more than occasionally. As a result, the place of employment, home, and general social areas offer extreme comfort for any individual.

Instant communication is possible no matter where one is located. Simply calling out someone's name is sufficient to initiate a near-instantaneous, pictographic, and real-time conversation. The feature can be disconnected for periods of privacy. Food processors are available in many locations, and are capable of providing a preselected diet that has already been programmed for specific individuals. All doors and windows open automatically by gentle touch. At home, they respond only to the touch of those residing there.

Transportation is automatically activated on command by any human, as are all service modules, such as public bathrooms, moving walkways, beverage dispensers, etc.

There are a number of different forms of transportation, the most important being local. This includes electromagnetic elevators, underground tubes, moving walkways, and teletransporters that can move a person from one town to another almost instantaneously. These are all voice- or touch-operated and free of charge.

Travel between cities is possible in two ways. Hover cars are used for vacations and sightseeing, and are considered an adventure. The other is the teletransporter, a machine that pulls space/time from one place to the next. Whatever happens to be contained in that space/time location is moved. The size of the area can be modulated on command, so that it will accommodate either a single person or a group of people being transported. Its physical range is limited only by the power feed. Small machines about the size of today's phone booth are good for intracity movement (within a single city—street to street.)

Larger machines, about the size of a bus, are intercity capable (can move one or a group of individuals from city to city). Mainframe teletransporters are located in central cities and are used for transport between planets within the solar system, Earth to Mars, Mars to the Moon, and return trips.

The ultimate transporters are the ships. These are singularities that are kept in orbit, and are small realities unto themselves. Once you have been transported to one of these ships, it is capable of crossing the universe, visiting any galaxy desired. The only problem is, they are still experimental in the year 3000. Mapping and controlling a fourth-dimensional location in space/time over vast distances is a brand-new science that is still being learned. Local travel is difficult enough, but because the differences in time are so minute, there's no getting lost locally—even between planets. Time differences over the vastness of the universe is a whole different matter. Teams of explorers have been literally "lost in space."

The discovery and development of this new technology has opened a new chapter in human culture and evolution, which actually began as far back as our own time—the twenty-first century. But the history books of the future will tell us that because of our primitive and less-than-desirable behavior traits, no one wanted any formal contact with us beyond an acknowledgement of our existence. So formal contact did not take place until well into the middle of the twenty-second century.

It was up to us to ferret out the way and means of joining the others. By the year 3000, we will be well on our way to doing so. Under our own power, using our own capabilities, and as equals, we will be joining the other sentient beings who occupy space. It will be a long and interesting journey in finally getting to that very special point in space/time.

About the Author

Having been tested extensively under strict laboratory conditions, Joseph McMoneagle is considered to be one of the best and most consistent remote viewers in the world today.

As an originating member of what became known as Project STARGATE, McMoneagle provided remote viewing support to the CIA, DIA, NSA, DEA, Secret Service, FBI, United States Customs, the National Security Council, and most of the major commands in the Department of Defense from 1978 through 1995. He was an advisor and consultant in the paranormal to the Commanding General, United States Army Intelligence and Security Command (INSCOM), as well as the Army Chief of Staff for Intelligence (ACSI). In 1984, he was awarded a *Legion of Merit* for his remote viewing support to the nation's intelligence community, for "producing crucial and vital intelligence unavailable from any other source."

The owner and director of Intuitive Intelligence Applications, Inc., McMoneagle has been involved for thirty one years in the technical, paranormal, and social sciences fields. He is a full-time research associate with the Laboratories for Fundamental Research, Cognitive Sciences Laboratory, in Palo Alto, California, where he has provided support to remote viewing research and development since 1984. He was a consultant and remote viewer with SRI-International and Science Applications International Corporation from 1984 through 1995, and is a contributing member of the Parapsychological Association.

McMoneagle resides with his wife Nancy in the foothills of Virginia's Blue Ridge Mountains. He is working on his third book, which he states "must remain classified" until its release in 1999.

Hampton Roads Publishing Company

. . . for the evolving human spirit

Hampton Roads Publishing Company
publishes books on a variety of subjects including
metaphysics, health, complementary medicine,
visionary fiction, and other related topics.

For a copy of our latest catalog,
call toll-free, 800-766-8009,
or send your name and address to:

Hampton Roads Publishing Company
134 Burgess Lane
Charlottesville, VA 22902
e-mail: hrpc@hrpub.com
www.hrpub.com